DAN-79   DANTES SUBJECT STANDARDIZED TESTS (DSST)

This is your
PASSBOOK for...

History (Rise and Fall) of the Soviet Union

Test Preparation Study Guide
Questions & Answers

COPYRIGHT NOTICE

This book is SOLELY intended for, is sold ONLY to, and its use is RESTRICTED to individual, bona fide applicants or candidates who qualify by virtue of having seriously filed applications for appropriate license, certificate, professional and/or promotional advancement, higher school matriculation, scholarship, or other legitimate requirements of education and/or governmental authorities.

This book is NOT intended for use, class instruction, tutoring, training, duplication, copying, reprinting, excerption, or adaptation, etc., by:

1) Other publishers
2) Proprietors and/or Instructors of "Coaching" and/or Preparatory Courses
3) Personnel and/or Training Divisions of commercial, industrial, and governmental organizations
4) Schools, colleges, or universities and/or their departments and staffs, including teachers and other personnel
5) Testing Agencies or Bureaus
6) Study groups which seek by the purchase of a single volume to copy and/or duplicate and/or adapt this material for use by the group as a whole without having purchased individual volumes for each of the members of the group
7) Et al.

Such persons would be in violation of appropriate Federal and State statutes.

PROVISION OF LICENSING AGREEMENTS – Recognized educational, commercial, industrial, and governmental institutions and organizations, and others legitimately engaged in educational pursuits, including training, testing, and measurement activities, may address request for a licensing agreement to the copyright owners, who will determine whether, and under what conditions, including fees and charges, the materials in this book may be used them. In other words, a licensing facility exists for the legitimate use of the material in this book on other than an individual basis. However, it is asseverated and affirmed here that the material in this book CANNOT be used without the receipt of the express permission of such a licensing agreement from the Publishers. Inquiries re licensing should be addressed to the company, attention rights and permissions department.

All rights reserved, including the right of reproduction in whole or in part, in any form or by any means, electronic or mechanical, including photocopying, recording, or by any information storage and retrieval system, without permission in writing from the Publisher.

Copyright © 2024 by
National Learning Corporation

212 Michael Drive, Syosset, NY 11791
(516) 921-8888 • www.passbooks.com
E-mail: info@passbooks.com

PUBLISHED IN THE UNITED STATES OF AMERICA

PASSBOOK® SERIES

THE *PASSBOOK® SERIES* has been created to prepare applicants and candidates for the ultimate academic battlefield – the examination room.

At some time in our lives, each and every one of us may be required to take an examination – for validation, matriculation, admission, qualification, registration, certification, or licensure.

Based on the assumption that every applicant or candidate has met the basic formal educational standards, has taken the required number of courses, and read the necessary texts, the *PASSBOOK® SERIES* furnishes the one special preparation which may assure passing with confidence, instead of failing with insecurity. Examination questions – together with answers – are furnished as the basic vehicle for study so that the mysteries of the examination and its compounding difficulties may be eliminated or diminished by a sure method.

This book is meant to help you pass your examination provided that you qualify and are serious in your objective.

The entire field is reviewed through the huge store of content information which is succinctly presented through a provocative and challenging approach – the question-and-answer method.

A climate of success is established by furnishing the correct answers at the end of each test.

You soon learn to recognize types of questions, forms of questions, and patterns of questioning. You may even begin to anticipate expected outcomes.

You perceive that many questions are repeated or adapted so that you can gain acute insights, which may enable you to score many sure points.

You learn how to confront new questions, or types of questions, and to attack them confidently and work out the correct answers.

You note objectives and emphases, and recognize pitfalls and dangers, so that you may make positive educational adjustments.

Moreover, you are kept fully informed in relation to new concepts, methods, practices, and directions in the field.

You discover that you are actually taking the examination all the time: you are preparing for the examination by "taking" an examination, not by reading extraneous and/or supererogatory textbooks.

In short, this PASSBOOK®, used directedly, should be an important factor in helping you to pass your test.

NONTRADITIONAL EDUCATION

Students returning to school as adults bring more varied experience to their studies than do the teenagers who begin college shortly after graduating from high school. As a result, there are numerous programs for students with nontraditional learning curves. Hundreds of colleges and universities grant degrees to people who cannot attend classes at a regular campus or have already learned what the college is supposed to teach.

You can earn nontraditional education credits in many ways:
- Passing standardized exams
- Demonstrating knowledge gained through experience
- Completing campus-based coursework, and
- Taking courses off campus

Some methods of assessing learning for credit are objective, such as standardized tests. Others are more subjective, such as a review of life experiences.

With some help from four hypothetical characters – Alice, Vin, Lynette, and Jorge – this article describes nontraditional ways of earning educational credit. It begins by describing programs in which you can earn a high school diploma without spending 4 years in a classroom. The college picture is more complicated, so it is presented in two parts: one on gaining credit for what you know through course work or experience, and a second on college degree programs. The final section lists resources for locating more information.

Earning High School Credit

People who were prevented from finishing high school as teenagers have several options if they want to do so as adults. Some major cities have back-to-school programs that allow adults to attend high school classes with current students. But the more practical alternatives for most adults are to take the General Educational Development (GED) tests or to earn a high school diploma by demonstrating their skills or taking correspondence classes.

Of course, these options do not match the experience of staying in high school and graduating with one's friends. But they are viable alternatives for adult learners committed to meeting and, often, continuing their educational goals.

GED Program

Alice quit high school her sophomore year and took a job to help support herself, her younger brother, and their newly widowed mother. Now an adult, she wants to earn her high school diploma – and then go on to college. Because her job as head cook and her family responsibilities keep her busy during the day, she plans to get a high school equivalency diploma. She will study for, and take, the GED tests. Every year, about half a million adults earn their high school credentials this way. A GED diploma is accepted in lieu of a high school one by more than 90 percent of employers, colleges, and universities, so it is a good choice for someone like Alice.

The GED testing program is sponsored by the American Council on Education and State and local education departments. It consists of examinations in five subject areas: Writing, science, mathematics, social studies, and literature and the arts. The tests also measure skills such as analytical ability, problem solving, reading comprehension, and ability to understand and apply information. Most of the questions are multiple choice; the writing test includes an essay section on a topic of general interest.

Eligibility rules for taking the exams vary, but some states require that you must be at least 18. Tests are given in English, Spanish, and French. In addition to standard print, versions in large print, Braille, and audiocassette are also available. Total time allotted for the tests is 7 1/2 hours.

The GED tests are not easy. About one-fourth of those who complete the exams every year do not pass. Passing scores are established by administering the tests to a sample of graduating high school seniors. The minimum standard score is set so that about one-third of graduating seniors would not pass the tests if they took them.

Because of the difficulty of the tests, people need to prepare themselves to take them. Often, they start by taking the Official GED Practice Tests, usually available through a local adult education center. Centers are listed in your phone book's blue pages under "Adult Education," "Continuing Education," or "GED." Adult education centers also have information about GED preparation classes and self-study materials. Classes are generally arranged to accommodate adults' work schedules. National Learning Corporation publishes several study guides that aim to thoroughly prepare test-takers for the GED.

School districts, colleges, adult education centers, and community organizations have information about GED testing schedules and practice tests. For more information, contact them, your nearest GED testing center, or:
GED Testing Service
One Dupont Circle, NW, Suite 250
Washington, DC 20036-1163
1(800) 62-MY GED (626-9433)
(202) 939-9490

Skills Demonstration

Adults who have acquired high school level skills through experience might be eligible for the National External Diploma Program. This alternative to the GED does not involve any direct instruction. Instead, adults seeking a high school diploma must demonstrate mastery of 65 competencies in 8 general areas: Communication; computation; occupational preparedness; and self, social, consumer, scientific, and technological awareness.

Mastery is shown through the completion of the tasks. For example, a participant could prove competency in computation by measuring a room for carpeting, figuring out the amount of carpet needed, and computing the cost.

Before being accepted for the program, adults undergo an evaluation. Tests taken at one of the program's offices measure reading, writing, and mathematics abilities. A take-home segment includes a self-assessment of current skills, an individual skill evaluation, and an occupational interest and aptitude test.

Adults accepted for the program have weekly meetings with an assessor. At the meeting, the assessor reviews the participant's work from the previous week. If the task has not been completed properly, the assessor explains the mistake. Participants continue to correct their errors until they master each competency. A high school diploma is awarded upon proven mastery of all 65 competencies.

Fourteen States and the District of Columbia now offer the External Diploma Program. For more information, contact:

External Diploma Program
One Dupont Circle, NW, Suite 250
Washington, DC 20036-1193
(202) 939-9475

Correspondence and Distance Study

Vin dropped out of high school during his junior year because his family's frequent moves made it difficult for him to continue his studies. He promised himself at the time he dropped out that he would someday finish the courses needed for his diploma. For people like Vin, who prefer to earn a traditional diploma in a nontraditional way, there are about a dozen accredited courses of study for earning a high school diploma by correspondence, or distance study. The programs are either privately run, affiliated with a university, or administered by a State education department.

Distance study diploma programs have no residency requirements, allowing students to continue their studies from almost any location. Depending on the course of study, students need not be enrolled full time and usually have more flexible schedules for finishing their work. Selection of courses ranges from vo-tech to college prep, and some programs place different emphasis on the types of diplomas offered. University affiliated schools, for example, allow qualified students to take college courses along with their high school ones. Students can then apply the college credits toward a degree at that university or transfer them to another institution.

Taking courses by distance study is often more challenging and time consuming than attending classes, especially for adults who have other obligations. Success depends on each student's motivation. Students usually do reading assignments on their own. Written exercises, which they complete and send to an instructor for grading, supplement their reading material.

A list of some accredited high schools that offer diplomas by distance study is available free from the Distance Education and Training Council, formerly known as the National Home Study Council. Request the "DETC Directory of Accredited Institutions" from:

The Distance Education and Training Council
1601 18th Street, NW.
Washington, DC 20009-2529
(202) 234-5100

Some publications profiling nontraditional college programs include addresses and descriptions of several high school correspondence ones. See the Resources section at the end of this article for more information.

Getting College Credit For What You Know

Adults can receive college credit for prior coursework, by passing examinations, and documenting experiential learning. With help from a college advisor, nontraditional students should assess their skills, establish their educational goals, and determine the number of college credits they might be eligible for.

Even before you meet with a college advisor, you should collect all your school and training records. Then, make a list of all knowledge and abilities acquired through experience, no matter how irrelevant they seem to your chosen field. Next, determine your educational goals: What specific field do you wish to study? What kind of a degree do you want? Finally, determine how your past work fits into the field of study. Later on, you will evaluate educational programs to find one that's right for you.

People who have complex educational or experiential learning histories might want to have their learning evaluated by the Regents Credit Bank. The Credit Bank, operated by Regents College of the University of the State of New York, allows people to consolidate credits earned through college, experience, or other methods. Special assessments are available for Regents College enrollees whose knowledge in a specific field cannot be adequately evaluated by standardized exams. For more information, contact the Regents Credit Bank at:

Regents College
7 Columbia Circle
Albany, NY 12203-5159
(518) 464-8500

Credit For Prior College Coursework

When Lynette was in college during the 1970s, she attended several different schools and took a variety of courses. She did well in some classes and poorly in others. Now that she is a successful business owner and has more focus, Lynette thinks she should forget about her previous coursework and start from scratch. Instead, she should start from where she is.

Lynette should have all her transcripts sent to the colleges or universities of her choice and let an admissions officer determine which classes are applicable toward a degree. A few credits here and there may not seem like much, but they add up. Even if the subjects do not seem relevant to any major, they might be counted as elective credits toward a degree. And comparing the cost of transcripts with the cost of college courses, it makes sense to spend a few dollars per transcript for a chance to save hundreds, and perhaps thousands, of dollars in books and tuition.

Rules for transferring credits apply to all prior coursework at accredited colleges and universities, whether done on campus or off. Courses completed off campus, often called extended learning, include those available to students through independent study and correspondence. Many schools have extended learning programs; Brigham Young University, for example, offers more than 300 courses through its Department of Independent Study. One type of extended learning is distance learning, a form of correspondence study by technological means such as television, video and audio, CD-ROM, electronic mail, and computer tutorials. See the Resources section at the end of this article for more information about publications available from the National University Continuing Education Association.

Any previously earned college credits should be considered for transfer, no matter what the subject or the grade received. Many schools do not accept the transfer of courses graded below a C or ones taken more than a designated number of years ago. Some colleges and universities also have limits on the number of credits that can be transferred and applied toward a degree. But not all do. For example, Thomas Edison State College, New Jersey's State college for adults, accepts the transfer of all 120 hours of credit required for a baccalaureate degree – provided all the credits are transferred from regionally accredited schools, no more than 80 are at the junior college level, and the student's grades overall and in the field of study average out to C.

To assign credit for prior coursework, most schools require original transcripts. This means you must complete a form or send a written, signed request to have your transcripts released directly to a college or university. Once you have chosen the schools you want to apply to, contact the schools you attended before. Find out how much each transcript costs, and ask them to send your transcripts to the ones you are applying to. Write a letter that includes your name (and names used during attendance, if different) and dates of attendance, along with the names and addresses of the schools to which your transcripts should be sent. Include payment and mail to the registrar at the schools you have attended. The registrar's office will process your request and send an official transcript of your coursework to the colleges or universities you have designated.

Credit For Noncollege Courses

Colleges and universities are not the only ones that offer classes. Volunteer organizations and employers often provide formal training worth college credit. The American Council on Education has two programs that assess thousands of specific courses and make recommendations on the amount of college credit they are worth. Colleges and universities accept the recommendations or use them as guidelines.

One program evaluates educational courses sponsored by government agencies, business and industry, labor unions, and professional and voluntary organizations. It is the Program on Noncollegiate Sponsored Instruction (PONSI). Some of the training seminars Alice has participated in covered topics such as food preparation, kitchen safety, and nutrition. Although she has not yet earned her GED, Alice can earn college credit because of her completion of these formal job-training seminars. The number of credits each seminar is worth does not hinge on Alice's current eligibility for college enrollment.

The other program evaluates courses offered by the Army, Navy, Air Force, Marines, Coast Guard, and Department of Defense. It is the Military Evaluations Program. Jorge has never attended college, but the engineering technology classes he completed as part of his military training are worth college credit. And as an Army veteran, Jorge is eligible for a service that takes the evaluations one step further. The Army/American Council on Education Registry Transcript System (AARTS) will provide Jorge with an individualized transcript of American Council on Education credit recommendations for all courses he completed, the military occupational specialties (MOS's) he held, and examinations he passed while in the Army. All Army and National Guard enlisted personnel and veterans who enlisted after October 1981 are eligible for the transcript. Similar services are being considered by the Navy and Marine Corps.

To obtain a free transcript, see your Army Education Center for a 5454R transcript request form. Include your name, Social Security number, basic active service date, and complete address where you want the transcript sent. Mail your request to:

AARTS Operations Center
415 McPherson Ave.
Fort Leavenworth, KS 66027-1373

Recommendations for PONSI are published in *The National Guide to Educational Credit for Training Programs;* military program recommendations are in *The Guide to the Evaluation of Educational Experiences in the Armed Forces.* See the Resources section at the end of this article for more information about these publications.

Former military personnel who took a foreign language course through the Defense Language Institute may request course transcripts by sending their name, Social Security number, course title, duration of the course, and graduation date to:

Commandant, Defense Language Institute
Attn: ATFL-DAA-AR
Transcripts
Presidio of Monterey
Monterey, CA 93944-5006

Not all of Jorge's and Alice's courses have been assessed by the American Council on Education. Training courses that have no Council credit recommendation should still be assessed by an advisor at the schools they want to attend. Course descriptions, class notes, test scores, and other documentation may be helpful for comparing training courses to their college equivalents. An oral examination or other demonstration of competency might also be required.

There is no guarantee you will receive all the credits you are seeking – but you certainly won't if you make no attempt.

Credit By Examination

Standardized tests are the best-known method of receiving college credit without taking courses. These exams are often taken by high school students seeking advanced placement for college, but they are also available to adult learners. Testing programs and colleges and universities offer exams in a number of subjects. Two U.S. Government institutes have foreign language exams for employees that also may be worth college credit.

It is important to understand that receiving a passing score on these exams does not mean you get college credit automatically. Each school determines which test results it will accept, minimum scores required, how scores are converted for credit, and the amount of credit, if any, to be assigned. Most colleges and universities accept the American Council on Education credit recommendations, published every other year in the 250-page *Guide to Educational Credit by Examination*. For more information, contact:

The American Council on Education
Credit by Examination Program
One Dupont Circle, Suite 250
Washington, DC 20036-1193
(202) 939-9434

Testing programs:

You might know some of the five national testing programs by their acronyms or initials: CLEP, ACT PEP: RCE, DANTES, AP, and NOCTI. (The meanings of these initialisms are explained below.) There is some overlap among programs; for example, four of them have introductory accounting exams. Since you will not be awarded credit more than once for a specific subject, you should carefully evaluate each program for the subject exams you wish to take. And before taking an exam, make sure you will be awarded credit by the college or university you plan to attend.

CLEP (College-Level Examination Program), administered by the College Board, is the most widely accepted of the national testing programs; more than 2,800 accredited schools award credit for passing exam scores. Each test covers material taught in basic undergraduate courses. There are five general exams – English composition, humanities, college mathematics, natural sciences, and social sciences and history – and many subject exams. Most exams are entirely multiple-choice, but English composition exams may include an essay section. For more information, contact:

    CLEP
    P.O. Box 6600
    Princeton, NJ 08541-6600
    (609) 771-7865

ACT PEP: RCE (American College Testing Proficiency Exam Program: Regents College Examinations) tests are given in 38 subjects within arts and sciences, business, education, and nursing. Each exam is recommended for either lower- or upper-level credit. Exams contain either objective or extended response questions, and are graded according to a standard score, letter grade, or pass/fail. Fees vary, depending on the subject and type of exam. For more information or to request free study guides, contact:

    ACT PEP: Regents College Examinations
    P.O. Box 4014
    Iowa City, IA 52243
    (319) 337-1387
    (New York State residents must contact Regents College directly.)

DANTES (Defense Activity for Nontraditional Education Support) standardized tests are developed by the Educational Testing Service for the Department of Defense. Originally administered only to military personnel, the exams have been available to the public since 1983. About 50 subject tests cover business, mathematics, social science, physical science, humanities, foreign languages, and applied technology. Most of the tests consist entirely of multiple-choice questions. Schools determine their own administering fees and testing schedules. For more information or to request free study sheets, contact:

    DANTES Program Office
    Mail Stop 31-X
    Educational Testing Service
    Princeton, NJ 08541
    1(800) 257-9484

The AP (Advanced Placement) Program is a cooperative effort between secondary schools and colleges and universities. AP exams are developed each year by committees of college and high school faculty appointed by the College Board and assisted by consultants from the Educational Testing Service. Subjects include arts and languages, natural sciences, computer science, social sciences, history, and mathematics. Most tests are 2 or 3 hours long and include both multiple-choice and essay questions. AP courses are available to help students prepare for exams, which are offered in the spring. For more information about the Advanced Placement Program, contact:

    Advanced Placement Services
    P.O. Box 6671
    Princeton, NJ 08541-6671
    (609) 771-7300

NOCTI (National Occupational Competency Testing Institute) assessments are designed for people like Alice, who have vocational-technical skills that cannot be evaluated by other tests. NOCTI assesses competency at two levels: Student/job ready and teacher/experienced worker. Standardized evaluations are available for occupations such as auto-body repair, electronics, mechanical drafting, quantity food preparation, and upholstering. The tests consist of multiple-choice questions and a performance component. Other services include workshops, customized assessments, and pre-testing. For more information, contact:
NOCTI
500 N. Bronson Ave.
Ferris State University
Big Rapids, MI 49307
(616) 796-4699

Colleges and universities:

Many colleges and universities have credit-by-exam programs, through which students earn credit by passing a comprehensive exam for a course offered by the institution. Among the most widely recognized are the programs at Ohio University, the University of North Carolina, Thomas Edison State College, and New York University.

Ohio University offers about 150 examinations for credit. In addition, you may sometimes arrange to take special examinations in non-laboratory courses offered at Ohio University. To take a test for credit, you must enroll in the course. If you plan to transfer the credit earned, you also need written permission from an official at your school. Books and study materials are available, for a cost, through the university. Exams must be taken within 6 months of the enrollment date; most last 3 hours. You may arrange to take the exam off campus if you do not live near the university.

Ohio University is on the quarter-hour system; most courses are worth 4 quarter hours, the equivalent of 3 semester hours. For more information, contact:
Independent Study
Tupper Hall 302
Ohio University
Athens, OH 45701-2979
1(800) 444-2910
(614) 593-2910

The University of North Carolina offers a credit-by-examination option for 140 independent study (correspondence) courses in foreign languages, humanities, social sciences, mathematics, business administration, education, electrical and computer engineering, health administration, and natural sciences. To take an exam, you must request and receive approval from both the course instructor and the independent studies department. Exams must be taken within six months of enrollment, and you may register for no more than two at a time. If you are not near the University's Chapel Hill campus, you may take your exam under supervision at an accredited college, university, community college, or technical institute. For more information, contact:
Independent Studies
CB #1020, The Friday Center
UNC-Chapel Hill
Chapel Hill, NC 27599-1020
1(800) 862-5669 / (919) 962-1134

The Thomas Edison College Examination Program offers more than 50 exams in liberal arts, business, and professional areas. Thomas Edison State College administers tests twice a month in Trenton, New Jersey; however, students may arrange to take their tests with a proctor at any accredited American college or university or U.S. military base. Most of the tests are multiple choice; some also include short answer or essay questions. Time limits range from 90 minutes to 4 hours, depending on the exam. For more information, contact:

Thomas Edison State College
TECEP, Office of Testing and Assessment
101 W. State Street
Trenton, NJ 08608-1176
(609) 633-2844

New York University's Foreign Language Program offers proficiency exams in more than 40 languages, from Albanian to Yiddish. Two exams are available in each language: The 12-point test is equivalent to 4 undergraduate semesters, and the 16-point exam may lead to upper level credit. The tests are given at the university's Foreign Language Department throughout the year.

Proof of foreign language proficiency does not guarantee college credit. Some colleges and universities accept transcripts only for languages commonly taught, such as French and Spanish. Nontraditional programs are more likely than traditional ones to grant credit for proficiency in other languages.

For an informational brochure and registration form for NYU's foreign language proficiency exams, contact:

New York University
Foreign Language Department
48 Cooper Square, Room 107
New York, NY 10003
(212) 998-7030

Government institutes:
The Defense Language Institute and Foreign Service Institute administer foreign language proficiency exams for personnel stationed abroad. Usually, the tests are given at the end of intensive language courses or upon completion of service overseas. But some people – like Jorge, who knows Spanish – speak another language fluently and may be allowed to take a proficiency exam in that language before completing their tour of duty. Contact one of the offices listed below to obtain transcripts of those scores. Proof of proficiency does not guarantee college credit, however, as discussed above.

To request score reports from the Defense Language Institute for Defense Language Proficiency Tests, send your name, Social Security number, language for which you were tested, and, most importantly, when and where you took the exam to:

Commandant, Defense Language Institute
Attn: ATFL-ES-T
DLPT Score Report Request
Presidio of Monterey
Monterey, CA 93944-5006

To request transcripts of scores for Foreign Service Institute exams, send your name, Social Security number, language for which you were tested, and dates or year of exams to:

Foreign Service Institute
Arlington Hall
4020 Arlington Boulevard
Rosslyn, VA 22204-1500
Attn: Testing Office (Send your request to the attention of the testing office of the foreign language in which you were tested)

Credit For Experience

Experiential learning credit may be given for knowledge gained through job responsibilities, personal hobbies, volunteer opportunities, homemaking, and other experiences. Colleges and universities base credit awards on the knowledge you have attained, not for the experience alone. In addition, the knowledge must be college level; not just any learning will do. Throwing horseshoes as a hobby is not likely to be worth college credit. But if you've done research on how and where the sport originated, visited blacksmiths, organized tournaments, and written a column for a trade journal — well, that's a horseshoe of a different color.

Adults attempting to get credit for their experience should be forewarned: Having your experience evaluated for college credit is time-consuming, tedious work — not an easy shortcut for people who want quick-fix college credits. And not all experience, no matter how valuable, is the equivalent of college courses.

Requesting college credit for your experiential learning can be tricky. You should get assistance from a credit evaluations officer at the school you plan to attend, but you should also have a general idea of what your knowledge is worth. A common method for converting knowledge into credit is to use a college catalog. Find course titles and descriptions that match what you have learned through experience, and request the number of credits offered for those courses.

Once you know what credit to ask for, you must usually present your case in writing to officials at the college you plan to attend. The most common form of presenting experiential learning for credit is the portfolio. A portfolio is a written record of your knowledge along with a request for equivalent college credit. It includes an identification and description of the knowledge for which you are requesting credit, an explanatory essay of how the knowledge was gained and how it fits into your educational plans, documentation that you have acquired such knowledge, and a request for college credit. Required elements of a portfolio vary by schools but generally follow those guidelines.

In identifying knowledge you have gained, be specific about exactly what you have learned. For example, it is not enough for Lynette to say she runs a business. She must identify the knowledge she has gained from running it, such as personnel management, tax law, marketing strategy, and inventory review. She must also include brief descriptions about her knowledge of each to support her claims of having those skills.

The essay gives you a chance to relay something about who you are. It should address your educational goals, include relevant autobiographical details, and be well organized, neat, and convey confidence. In his essay, Jorge might first state his goal of becoming an engineer. Then he would explain why he joined the Army, where he got hands-on training and experience in developing and servicing electronic equipment.

This, he would say, led to his hobby of creating remote-controlled model cars, of which he has built 20. His conclusion would highlight his accomplishments and tie them to his desire to become an electronic engineer.

Documentation is evidence that you've learned what you claim to have learned. You can show proof of knowledge in a variety of ways, including audio or video recordings, letters from current or former employers describing your specific duties and job performance, blueprints, photographs or artwork, and transcripts of certifying exams for professional licenses and certification – such as Alice's certification from the American Culinary Federation. Although documentation can take many forms, written proof alone is not always enough. If it is impossible to document your knowledge in writing, find out if your experiential learning can be assessed through supplemental oral exams by a faculty expert.

Earning a College Degree

Nontraditional students often have work, family, and financial obligations that prevent them from quitting their jobs to attend school full time. Can they still meet their educational goals? Yes.

More than 150 accredited colleges and universities have nontraditional bachelor's degree programs that require students to spend little or no time on campus; over 300 others have nontraditional campus-based degree programs. Some of those schools, as well as most junior and community colleges, offer associate's degrees nontraditionally. Each school with a nontraditional course of study determines its own rules for awarding credit for prior coursework, exams, or experience, as discussed previously. Most have charges on top of tuition for providing these special services.

Several publications profile nontraditional degree programs; see the Resources section at the end of this article for more information. To determine which school best fits your academic profile and educational goals, first list your criteria. Then, evaluate nontraditional programs based on their accreditation, features, residency requirements, and expenses. Once you have chosen several schools to explore further, write to them for more information. Detailed explanations of school policies should help you decide which ones you want to apply to.

Get beyond the printed word – especially the glowing words each school writes about itself. Check out the schools you are considering with higher education authorities, alumni, employers, family members, and friends. If possible, visit the campus to talk to students and instructors and sit in on a few classes, even if you will be completing most or all of your work off campus. Ask school officials questions about such things as enrollment numbers, graduation rate, faculty qualifications, and confusing details about the application process or academic policies. After you have thoroughly investigated each prospective college or university, you can make an informed decision about which is right for you.

Accreditation

Accreditation is a process colleges and universities submit to voluntarily for getting their credentials. An accredited school has been investigated and visited by teams of observers and has periodic inspections by a private accrediting agency. The initial review can take two years or more.

Regional agencies accredit entire schools, and professional agencies accredit either specialized schools or departments within schools. Although there are no national accrediting standards, not just any accreditation will do. Countless "accreditation associations" have been invented by schools, many of which have no academic programs and sell phony degrees, to accredit themselves. But 6 regional and about 80 professional accrediting associations in the United States are recognized by the U.S. Department of Education or the Commission on Recognition of Postsecondary Accreditation. When checking accreditation, these are the names to look for. For more information about accreditation and accrediting agencies, contact:

    Institutional Participation Oversight Service Accreditation and State Liaison Division
    U.S. Department of Education
    ROB 3, Room 3915
    600 Independence Ave., SW
    Washington, DC 20202-5244
    (202) 708-7417

Because accreditation is not mandatory, lack of accreditation does not necessarily mean a school or program is bad. Some schools choose not to apply for accreditation, are in the process of applying, or have educational methods too unconventional for an accrediting association's standards. For the nontraditional student, however, earning a degree from a college or university with recognized accreditation is an especially important consideration. Although nontraditional education is becoming more widely accepted, it is not yet mainstream. Employers skeptical of a degree earned in a nontraditional manner are likely to be even less accepting of one from an unaccredited school.

Program Features

Because nontraditional students have diverse educational objectives, nontraditional schools are diverse in what they offer. Some programs are geared toward helping students organize their scattered educational credits to get a degree as quickly as possible. Others cater to those who may have specific credits or experience but need assistance in completing requirements. Whatever your educational profile, you should look for a program that works with you in obtaining your educational goals.

A few nontraditional programs have special admissions policies for adult learners like Alice, who plan to earn their GEDs but want to enroll in college in the meantime. Other features of nontraditional programs include individualized learning agreements, intensive academic counseling, cooperative learning and internship placement, and waiver of some prerequisites or other requirements – as well as college credit for prior coursework, examinations, and experiential learning, all discussed previously.

Lynette, whose primary goal is to finish her degree, wants to earn maximum credits for her business experience. She will look for programs that do not limit the number of credits awarded for equivalency exams and experiential learning. And since well-documented proof of knowledge is essential for earning experiential learning credits, Lynette should make sure the program she chooses provides assistance to students submitting a portfolio.

Jorge, on the other hand, has more credits than he needs in certain areas and is willing to forego some. To become an engineer, he must have a bachelor's degree; but because he is accustomed to hands-on learning, Jorge is interested in getting experience as he gains more technical skills. He will concentrate on finding schools with strong cooperative education, supervised fieldwork, or internship programs.

Residency Requirements

Programs are sometimes deemed nontraditional because of their residency requirements. Many people think of residency for colleges and universities in terms of tuition, with in-state students paying less than out-of-state ones. Residency also may refer to where a student lives, either on or off campus, while attending school.

But in nontraditional education, residency usually refers to how much time students must spend on campus, regardless of whether they attend classes there. In some nontraditional programs, students need not ever step foot on campus. Others require only a very short residency, such as one day or a few weeks. Many schools have standard residency requirements of several semesters but schedule classes for evenings or weekends to accommodate working adults.

Lynette, who previously took courses by independent study, prefers to earn credits by distance study. She will focus on schools that have no residency requirement. Several colleges and universities have nonresident degree completion programs for adults with some college credit. Under the direction of a faculty advisor, students devise a plan for earning their remaining credits. Methods for earning credits include independent study, distance learning, seminars, supervised fieldwork, and group study at arranged sites. Students may have to earn a certain number of credits through the degree-granting institution. But many programs allow students to take courses at accredited schools of their choice for transfer toward their degree.

Alice wants to attend lectures but has an unpredictable schedule. Her best course of action will be to seek out short residency programs that require students to attend seminars once or twice a semester. She can take courses that are televised and videotape them to watch when her schedule permits, with the seminars helping to ensure that she properly completes her coursework. Many colleges and universities with short residency requirements also permit students to earn some credits elsewhere, by whatever means the student chooses.

Some fields of study require classroom instruction. As Jorge will discover, few colleges and universities allow students to earn a bachelor's degree in engineering entirely through independent study. Nontraditional residency programs are designed to accommodate adults' daytime work schedules. Jorge should look for programs offering evening, weekend, summer, and accelerated courses.

Tuition and Other Expenses

The final decisions about which schools Alice, Jorge, and Lynette attend may hinge in large part on a single issue: Cost. And rising tuition is only part of the equation. Beginning with application fees and continuing through graduation fees, college expenses add up.

Traditional and nontraditional students have some expenses in common, such as the cost of books and other materials. Tuition might even be the same for some courses, especially for colleges and universities offering standard ones at unusual times. But for nontraditional programs, students may also pay fees for services such as credit or transcript review, evaluation, advisement, and portfolio assessment.

Students are also responsible for postage and handling or setup expenses for independent study courses, as well as for all examination and transcript fees for transferring credits. Usually, the more nontraditional the program, the more detailed the fees. Some schools charge a yearly enrollment fee rather than tuition for degree completion candidates who want their files to remain active.

Although tuition and fees might seem expensive, most educators tell you not to let money come between you and your educational goals. Talk to someone in the financial aid department of the school you plan to attend or check your library for publications about financial aid sources. The U.S. Department of Education publishes a guide to Federal aid programs such as Pell Grants, student loans, and work-study. To order the free 74-page booklet, *The Student Guide: Financial Aid from the U.S. Department of Education,* contact:

Federal Student Aid Information Center
P.O. Box 84
Washington, DC 20044
1 (800) 4FED-AID (433-3243)

Resources

Information on how to earn a high school diploma or college degree without following the usual routes is available from several organizations and in numerous publications. Information on nontraditional graduate degree programs, available for master's through doctoral level, though not discussed in this article, can usually be obtained from the same resources that detail bachelor's degree programs.

National Learning Corporation publishes study guides for all of these exams, for both general examinations and tests in specific subject areas. To order study guides, or to browse their catalog featuring more than 5,000 titles, visit NLC online at www.passbooks.com, or contact them by phone at (800) 632-8888.

Organizations

Adult learners should always contact their local school system, community college, or university to learn about programs that are readily available. The following national organizations can also supply information:

American Council on Education
One Dupont Circle
Washington, DC 20036-1193
(202) 939-9300

Within the American Council on Education, the Center for Adult Learning and Educational Credentials administers the National External Diploma Program, the GED Program, the Program on Noncollegiate Sponsored Instruction, the Credit by Examination Program, and the Military Evaluations Program.

DANTES Subject Standardized Tests

INTRODUCTION

The DANTES (Defense Activity for Non-Traditional Education Support) subject standardized tests are comprehensive college and graduate level examinations given by the Armed Forces, colleges and graduate schools as end-of-subject course evaluation final examinations or to obtain college equivalency credits in the various subject areas tested.

The DANTES Examination Program enables students to obtain college credit for what they have learned on the job, through self-study, personal interest, correspondence courses or by any other means. It is used by colleges and universities to award college credit to students who demonstrate that they know as much as students completing an equivalent college course. It is a cost-efficient, time-saving way for students to use their knowledge to accomplish their educational goals.

Most schools accept the American Council on Education (ACE) recommendations for the minimum score required and the amount of credit awarded, but not all schools do. Be sure to check the policy regarding the score level required for credit and the number of credits to be awarded.

Not all tests are accepted by all institutions. Even when a test is accepted by an institution, it may not be acceptable for every program at that institution. Before considering testing, ascertain the acceptability of a specific test for a particular course.

Colleges and universities that administer DANTES tests may administer them to any applicant – or they may administer the tests only to students registered at their institution. Decisions about who will be allowed to test are made by the school. Students should contact the test center to determine current policies and schedules for DANTES testing.

Colleges and universities authorized to administer DANTES tests usually do so throughout the calendar year. Each school sets its own fee for test administration and establishes its own testing schedule. Contact the representative at the administering school directly to make arrangements for testing.

Checklist
For Students

- ✓ Visit **www.getcollegecredit.com** to obtain a list of tests, fact sheets, test preparation materials, participating colleges and universities, and much more.

- ✓ Contact your school advisor to confirm that the DSST you selected will fit into your curriculum.

- ✓ Consult the ***DSST Candidate Information Bulletin*** for answers to specific questions.

- ✓ Contact the test site to schedule your test.

- ✓ Prepare for your examination by using the fact sheet as a guide.

- ✓ Take the test.

If you would like a score report sent to your college or university, it is a good idea to bring the four-digit code with you. You must write the DSST Test Center Code for that institution on your answer sheet at the time of testing. DSST Test Center Codes are noted in the DSST Participating Colleges and Universities listing on the Web site.

If you prefer to send a score report to an institution at a later date, there is a transcript fee of $20 for each transcript ordered.

Thomson Prometric
DSST Program
2000 Lenox Drive, Third Floor
Lawrenceville, NJ 08648

Toll-free: 877-471-9860
609-895-5011

E-mail: pnj-dsst@thomson.com

MAKING A COLLEGE DEGREE WITHIN YOUR REACH

Today, there are many educational alternatives to the classroom—you can learn from your job, your reading, your independent study, and special interests you pursue. You may already have learned the subject matter covered by some college-level courses.

The DSST Program is a nationally recognized testing program that gives you the opportunity to receive college credit for learning acquired outside the traditional college classroom. Colleges and universities throughout the United States administer the program, developed by Thomson Prometric, year-round. Annually, over 90,000 DSSTs are administered to individuals who are interested in continuing their education. Take advantage of the DSST testing program; it speeds the educational process and provides the flexibility adults need, making earning a degree more feasible.

Since requirements differ from college to college, please check with the credit-awarding institution before taking a DSST. More than 1,800 colleges and universities currently award credit for DSSTs, and the number is growing every day. You can choose from 37 test titles in the areas of Social Science, Business, Mathematics, Applied Technology, Humanities, and Physical Science. A brief description of each examination is found on the pages that follow.

Reach Your Career Goals Through DSSTs

Use DSSTs to help you earn your degree, get a promotion, or simply demonstrate that you have college-level knowledge in subjects relevant to your work.

Save Time...

You don't have to sit through classes when you have previously acquired the knowledge or experience for most of what is being taught and can learn the rest yourself. You might be able to bypass introductory-level courses in subject areas you already know.

Save Money...

DSSTs save you money because the classes you bypass by earning credit through the DSST Program are classes you won't have to pay for on your way to earning your degree. You can use the money instead to take more advanced courses that can be more challenging and rewarding.

Improve Your Chances for Admission to College

Each college has its own admission policies; however, having passing scores for DSSTs on your transcript can provide strong evidence of how well you can perform at the college level.

Gain Confidence Performing at a College Level

Many adults returning to college find that lack of confidence is often the greatest hurdle to overcome. Passing a DSST demonstrates your ability to perform on a college level.

Make Up for Courses You May Have Missed

You may be ready to graduate from college and find that you are a few credits short of earning your degree. By using semester breaks, vacation time, or leisure time to study independently, you can prepare to take one or more DSSTs, fulfill your academic requirements, and graduate on time.

If You Cannot Attend Regularly Scheduled Classes...

If your lifestyle or responsibilities prevent you from attending regularly scheduled classes, you can earn your college degree from a college offering an external degree program. The DSST Program allows you to earn your degree by study and experience outside the traditional classroom.

Many colleges and universities offer external degree or distance learning programs. For additional information, contact the college you plan to attend or:

Center for Lifelong Learning
American Council on Education
One DuPont Circle NW, Suite 250
Washington, DC 20036
202-939-9475
www.acenet.edu
(Select "Center for Lifelong Learning" under "Programs & Services"
for more information)

Fact Sheets

For each test, there is a Fact Sheet that outlines the topics covered by each test and includes a list of sample questions, a list of recommended references of books that would be useful for review, and the number of credits awarded for a passing score as recommended by the American Council on Education (ACE). *Please note that some schools require scores that are higher than the minimum ACE-recommended passing score.* It is suggested that you check with your college or university to determine what score they require in order to earn credit. You can obtain Fact Sheets by:
- Downloading them from www.getcollegecredit.com
- E-mailing a request to pnj-dsst@thomson.com
- Completing a Candidate Publications Order Form

DSST Online Practice Tests

DSST online practice tests contain items that reflect a *partial range of difficulty* identified in the Content Outline section on each Fact Sheet. There is an online DSST Practice Test in the following categories:
- Mathematics
- Social Science
- Business
- Physical Science
- Applied Technology
- Humanities

Although the online DSST Practice Test questions do not indicate the full range of difficulty you would find in an actual DSST test, they will help you assess your knowledge level. Each online DSST Practice Test can be purchased by visiting www.getcollegecredit.com and clicking on DSST Practice Exams.

TAKING DSST EXAMINATIONS

Earning College Credit for DSST Examinations
To find out if the college of your choice awards credit for passing DSST scores, contact the admissions office or counseling and testing office. The college can also provide information on the scores required for awarding credit, the number of credit hours awarded, and any courses that can be bypassed with satisfactory scores.

It is important that you contact the institution of your choice as early as possible since credit-awarding policies differ among colleges and universities.

Where to Take DSSTs
DSSTs are administered at colleges and universities nationwide. Each location determines the frequency and scheduling of test administrations. To obtain the most current list of participating DSST colleges and universities:
- Visit and download the information from www.getcollegecredit.com
- E-mail pnj-dsst@thomson.com

Scheduling Your Examination
Please be aware that some colleges and universities provide DSST testing services to enrolled students only. After you have selected a college or university that administers DSSTs, you will need to contact them to schedule your test date.

The fee to take a DSST is $60 per test. This fee entitles you to two score reports after the test is scored. One will be sent directly to you and the other will be sent to the college or university that you designate on your answer sheet. You may pay the test fee with a certified check or U.S. money order made payable to Thomson Prometric or you may charge the test fee to your Visa, MasterCard or American Express credit card. Note: The credit card statement will reflect a charge from Thomson Prometric for all DSST examinations. *(Declined credit card charges will be assessed an additional $25 processing fee.)*

In addition, the test site may also require a test administration fee for each examination, to be paid directly to the institution. Contact the test site to determine its administration fee and payment policy.

Other Testing Arrangements
If you are unable to find a participating DSST college or university in your area, you may want to contact the testing office of a local accredited college or university to determine whether a representative from that office will agree to administer the test(s) for you.

The school's representative should then contact the DSST Program at 866-794-3497 to arrange for this administration. If you are unable to locate a test site, contact Thomson Prometric for assistance at pnj-dsst@thomson.com or 866-794-3497.

Testing Accommodations for Students with Disabilities
Thomson Prometric is committed to serving test takers with disabilities by providing services and reasonable testing accommodations as set forth in the provisions of the *Americans with Disabilities Act* (ADA). If you have a disability, as prescribed by the ADA, and require special testing services or arrangements, please contact the test administrator at the test site. You will be asked to submit to the test administrator documentation of your disability and your request for special accommodations. The test

administrator will then forward your documentation along with your request for testing accommodations to Thomson Prometric for approval.

Please submit your request as far in advance of your test date as possible so that the necessary accommodations can be made. Only test takers with documented disabilities are eligible for special accommodations.

On the Day of the Examination

It is important to review this information and to have the correct identification present on the day of the examination:
- Arrive on time as a courtesy to the test administrator.
- Bring a valid form of government-issued identification that includes a current photo and your signature (acceptable documents include a driver's license, passport, state-issued identification card or military identification). *Anyone who fails to present valid identification will not be allowed to test.*
- Bring several No. 2 (soft-lead) sharpened pencils with good erasers, a watch, and a black pen if you will be writing an essay.
- Do not bring books or papers.
- Do not bring an alarm watch that beeps, a telephone, or a phone beeper into the testing room.
- The use of nonprogrammable calculators, slide rules, scratch paper and/or other materials is permitted for some of the tests.

DSST SCORING POLICIES

Your DSST examination scores are reported only to you, unless you request that they be sent elsewhere. If you want your scores sent to your college, you must provide the correct DSST code number of the school on your answer sheet at the time you take the test. See the *DSST Directory of Colleges and Universities* on the Web site www.getcollegecredit.com.

If your institution is not listed, contact Thomson Prometric at 866-794-3497 to establish a code number. (Some schools may require a student to be enrolled prior to receiving a score report.)

Receiving Your Score Report

Allow approximately four weeks after testing to receive your score report.

Calling DSST Customer Service before the required four-week score processing time has elapsed will not expedite the processing of your scores. Due to privacy and security requirements, scores will not be reported to students over the telephone under any circumstance.

Scoring of Principles of Public Speaking Speeches

The speech portion of the *Principles of Public Speaking* examination will be sent to speech raters who are faculty members at accredited colleges that currently teach or have previously taught the course. Scores for the *Principles of Public Speaking* examination are available six to eight weeks from receipt by Thomson Prometric. If you take the *Principles of Public Speaking* examination and fail (either the objective, speech portion, or both), you must follow the retesting policy waiting period of six months (180 days) before retaking the entire exam.

Essays

The essays for *Ethics in America* and *Technical Writing* are optional and thus are not scored by raters. The essays are forwarded to the college or university that you designate, along with your score report, for their use in determining the award of credit. Before taking the *Ethics in America* or *Technical Writing* examinations, check with your college or university to determine whether the essay is required.

NOTE: *Principles of Public Speaking* speech topic cassette tapes and essays are kept on file at Thomson Prometric for one year from the date of administration.

How to Get Transcripts

There is a $20 fee for each transcript you request. Payment must be in the form of a certified check, U.S. money order payable to Thomson Prometric, or credit card. Personal checks and debit cards are NOT an acceptable method of payment. One transcript may include scores for one or more examinations taken. To request a transcript, download the Transcript Order Form from www.getcollegecredit.com.

DESCRIPTION OF THE DSST EXAMINATIONS

Mathematics

- **Fundamentals of College Algebra** covers mathematical concepts such as fundamental algebraic operations; linear, absolute value; quadratic equations, inequalities, radials, exponents and logarithms, factoring polynomials and graphing. The use of a nonprogrammable, handheld calculator is permitted.

- **Principles of Statistics** tests the understanding of the various topics of statistics, both qualitatively and quantitatively, and the ability to apply statistical methods to solve a variety of problems. The topics included in this test are descriptive statistics; correlation and regression; probability; chance models and sampling and tests of significance. The use of a nonprogrammable, handheld calculator is permitted.

Social Science

- **Art of the Western World** deals with the history of art during the following periods: classical; Romanesque and Gothic; early Renaissance; high Renaissance, Baroque; rococo; neoclassicism and romanticism; realism, impressionism and post-impressionism; early twentieth century; and post-World War II.

- **Western Europe Since 1945** tests the knowledge of basic facts and terms and the understanding of concepts and principles related to the areas of the historical background of the aftermath of the Second World War and rebuilding of Europe; national political systems; issues and policies in Western European societies; European institutions and processes; and Europe's relations with the rest of the world.

- **An Introduction to the Modern Middle East** emphasizes core knowledge (including geography, Judaism, Christianity, Islam, ethnicity); nineteenth-century European impact; twentieth-century Western influences; World Wars I and II; new nations; social and cultural changes (1900-1960) and the Middle East from 1960 to present.

- **Human/Cultural Geography** includes the Earth and basic facts (coordinate systems, maps, physiography, atmosphere, soils and vegetation, water); culture and environment, spatial processes (social processes, modern economic systems, settlement patterns, political geography); and regional geography.

- **Rise and Fall of the Soviet Union** covers Russia under the Old Regime; the Revolutionary Period; New Economic Policy; Pre-war Stalinism; The Second World War; Post-war Stalinism; The Khrushchev Years; The Brezhnev Era; and reform and collapse.

- **A History of the Vietnam War** covers the history of the roots of the Vietnam War; the First Vietnam War (1946-1954); pre-war developments (1954-1963); American involvement in the Vietnam War; Tet (1968); Vietnamizing the War (1968-1973); Cambodia and Laos; peace; legacies and lessons.

- **The Civil War and Reconstruction** covers the Civil War from presecession (1861) through Reconstruction. It includes causes of the war; secession; Fort Sumter; the war in the east and in the west; major battles; the political situation; assassination of Lincoln; end of the Confederacy; and Reconstruction.

- **Foundations of Education** includes topics such as contemporary issues in education; past and current influences on education (philosophies, democratic ideals, social/economic influences); and the interrelationships between contemporary issues and influences.

- **Life-span Developmental Psychology** covers models and theories; methods of study; ethical issues; biological development; perception, learning and memory; cognition and language; social, emotional, and personality development; social behaviors, family life cycle, extrafamilial settings; singlehood and cohabitation; occupational development and retirement; adjustment to life stresses; and bereavement and loss.

- **Drug and Alcohol Abuse** includes such topics as drug use in society; classification of drugs; pharmacological principles; alcohol (types, effects of, alcoholism); general principles and use of sedative hypnotics, narcotic analgesics, stimulants, and hallucinogens; other drugs (inhalants, steroids); and prevention/treatment.

- **General Anthropology** deals with anthropology as a discipline; theoretical perspectives; physical anthropology; archaeology; social organization; economic organization; political organization; religion; and modernization and application of anthropology.

- **Introduction to Law Enforcement** includes topics such as history and professional movement of law enforcement; overview of the U.S. criminal justice system; police systems in the U.S.; police organization, management, and issues; and U.S. law and precedents.

- **Criminal Justice** deals with criminal behavior (crime in the U.S., theories of crime, types of crime); the criminal justice system (historical origins, legal foundations, due process); police; the court system (history and organization, adult court system, juvenile court, pre-trial and post-trial processes); and corrections.

- **Fundamentals of Counseling** covers historical development (significant influences and people); counselor roles and functions; the counseling relationship; and theoretical approaches to counseling.

Business
- **Principles of Finance** deals with financial statements and planning; time value of money; working capital management; valuation and characteristics; capital budgeting; cost of capital; risk and return; and international financial management. The use of a nonprogrammable, handheld calculator is permitted.

- **Principles of Financial Accounting** includes topics such as general concepts and principles, accounting cycle and classification; transaction analysis; accruals and deferrals; cash and internal control; current accounts; long- and short-term liabilities; capital stock; and financial statements. The use of a nonprogrammable, handheld calculator is permitted.

- **Human Resource Management** covers general employment issues; job analysis; training and development; performance appraisals; compensation issues; security issues; personnel legislation and regulation; labor relations and current issues; an overview of the Human Resource Management Field; Human Resource Planning; Staffing; training and development; compensation issues; safety and health; employee rights and discipline; employment law; labor relations and current issues and trends.

- **Organizational Behavior** deals with the study of organizational behavior (scientific approaches, research designs, data collection methods); individual processes and characteristics; interpersonal and group processes and characteristics; organizational processes and characteristics; and change and development processes.

- **Principles of Supervision** deals with the roles and responsibilities of the supervisor; management functions (planning, organization and staffing, directing at the supervisory level); and other topics (legal issues, stress management, union environments, quality concerns).

- **Business Law II** covers topics such as sales of goods; debtor and creditor relations; business organizations; property; and commercial paper.

- **Introduction to Computing** includes topics such as history and technological generations; hardware/software; applications to information technology; program development; data management; communications and connectivity; and computing and society. The use of a nonprogrammable, handheld calculator is permitted.

- **Management Information Systems** covers systems theory, analysis and design of systems, hardware and software; database management; telecommunications; management of the MIS functional area and informational support.

- **Introduction to Business** deals with economic issues affecting business; international business; government and business; forms of business ownership; small business, entrepreneurship and franchise; management process; human resource management; production and operations; marketing management; financial management; risk management and insurance; and management and information systems.

- **Money and Banking** covers the role and kinds of money; commercial banks and other financial intermediaries; central banking and the Federal Reserve system; money and macroeconomics activity; monetary policy in the U.S.; and the international monetary system.

- **Personal Finance** includes topics such as financial goals and values; budgeting; credit and debt; major purchases; taxes; insurance; investments; and retirement and estate planning. The use of auxiliary materials, such as calculators and slide rules, is NOT permitted.

- **Business Mathematics** deals with basic operations with integers, fractions, and decimals; round numbers; ratios; averages; business graphs; simple interest; compound interest and annuities; net pay and deductions; discounts and markups; depreciation and net worth; corporate securities; distribution of ownership; and stock and asset turnover.

Physical Science
• **Astronomy** covers the history of astronomy, celestial mechanics; celestial systems; astronomical instruments; the solar system; nature and evolution; the galaxy; the universe; determining astronomical distances; and life in the universe.

• **Here's to Your Health** covers mental health and behavior; human development and relationships; substance abuse; fitness and nutrition; risk factors, disease, and disease prevention; and safety, consumer awareness, and environmental concerns.

• **Environment and Humanity** deals with topics such as ecological concepts (ecosystems, global ecology, food chains and webs); environmental impacts; environmental management and conservation; and political processes and the future.

• **Principles of Physical Science I** includes physics: Newton's Laws of Motion; energy and momentum; thermodynamics; wave and optics; electricity and magnetism; chemistry: properties of matter; atomic theory and structure; and chemical reactions.

• **Physical Geology** covers Earth materials; igneous, sedimentary, and metamorphic rocks; surface processes (weathering, groundwater, glaciers, oceanic systems, deserts and winds, hydrologic cycle); internal Earth processes; and applications (mineral and energy resources, environmental geology).

Applied Technology
• **Technical Writing** covers topics such as theory and practice of technical writing; purpose, content, and organizational patterns of common types of technical documents; elements of various technical reports; and technical editing. Students have the option to write a short essay on one of the technical topics provided. Thomson Prometric will not score the essay; however, for determining the award of credit, a copy of the essay will be forwarded to the college or university you've designated along with the score report or transcript.

Humanities
• **Ethics in America** deals with ethical traditions (Greek views, Biblical traditions, moral law, consequential ethics, feminist ethics); ethical analysis of issues arising in interpersonal and personal-societal relationships and in professional and occupational roles; and relationships between ethical traditions and the ethical analysis of situations. Students have the option to write an essay to analyze a morally problematic situation in terms of issues relevant to a decision and arguments for alternative positions. Thomson Prometric will not score the essay; however, for determining the award of credit, a copy of the essay will be forwarded to the college or university you've designated along with the score report or transcript.

• **Introduction to World Religions** covers topics such as dimensions and approaches to religion; primal religions; Hinduism; Buddhism; Confucianism; Taoism; Judaism; Christianity; and Islam.

• **Principles of Public Speaking** consists of two parts: Part One consists of multiple-choice questions covering considerations of Principles of Public Speaking; audience analysis; purposes of speeches; structure/organization; content/supporting materials; research; language and style; delivery; communication apprehension; listening and feedback; and criticism and evaluation. Part Two requires the student to record an impromptu persuasive speech that will be scored.

FREQUENTLY ASKED QUESTIONS ABOUT DSSTs

In order to pass the test, must I study from one of the recommended references?
The recommended references are a listing of books that were being used as textbooks in college courses of the same or similar title at the time the test was developed. Appropriate textbooks for study are not limited to those listed in the fact sheet. If you wish to obtain study resources to prepare for the examination, you may reference either the current edition of the listed titles or textbooks currently used at a local college or university for the same class title. It is recommended that you reference more than one textbook on the topics outlined in the fact sheet. You should begin by checking textbook content against the content outline included on the front page of the DSST fact sheet before selecting textbooks that cover the text content from which to study. Textbooks may be found at the campus bookstore of a local college or university offering a course on the subject.

Is there a penalty for guessing on the tests?
There is no penalty for guessing on DSSTs, so you should mark an answer for each question.

How much time will I have to complete the test?
Many DSSTs can be completed within 90 minutes; however, additional time can be allowed if necessary.

What should I do if I find a test question irregularity?
Continue testing and then report the irregularity to the test administrator after the test. This may be done by asking that the test administrator note the irregularity on the Supervisor's Irregularity Report or you can write to Thomson Prometric, DSST Program, 2000 Lenox Drive, Third Floor, Lawrenceville, NJ 08648, and indicate the form and question number(s) or circumstances as well as your name and address.

When will I receive my score report?
Allow approximately four weeks from the date of testing to receive your score report. Allow six to eight weeks to receive a score report for the *Principles of Public Speaking* examination.

Will my test scores be released without my permission?
Your test score will not be released to anyone other than the school you designate on your answer sheet unless you write to us and ask us to send a transcript elsewhere. Instructions about how to do this can be found on your score report. Your scores may be used for research purposes, but individual scores are never made public nor are individuals identified if research findings are made public.

If I do not achieve a passing score on the test, how long must I wait until I can take the test again?
If you do not receive a score on the test that will enable you to obtain credit for the course, you may take the test again after six months (180 days). Please do not attempt to take the test before six months (180 days) have passed because you will receive a score report marked <u>invalid</u> and your test fee will not be refunded.

Can my test scores be canceled?

The test administrator is required to report any irregularities to Thomson Prometric. <u>The consequence of bringing unauthorized materials into the testing room, or giving or receiving help, will be the forfeiture of your test fee and the invalidation of test scores.</u> The DSST Program reserves the right to cancel scores and not issue score reports in such situations.

What can I do if I feel that my test scores were not accurately reported?

Thomson Prometric recognizes the extreme importance of test results to candidates and has a multi-step quality-control procedure to help ensure that reported scores are accurate. If you have reason to believe that your score(s) were not accurately reported, you may request to have your answer sheet reviewed and hand scored.

The fees for this service are:
- $20 fee if requested within six months of the test date
- $30 fee if requested more than six months from the test date
- $30 fee if a re-evaluation of the *Principles of Public Speaking* speech is requested

The fee for this service can be paid by credit card or by certified check or U.S. money order payable to Thomson Prometric. Submit your request for score verification along with the appropriate fee or credit card information (credit card number and expiration date) to Thomson Prometric, DSST Program, 2000 Lenox Drive, Third Floor, Lawrenceville, NJ 08648. Include your full name, the test title, the date you took the test, and your Social Security number. Candidates will be notified if a scoring discrepancy is discovered within four weeks of receipt of the request.

What does ACE recommendation mean?

The ACE recommendation is the minimum passing score recommended by the American Council on Education for any given test. It is equivalent to the average score of students in the DSST norming sample who received a grade of C for the course. Some schools require a score higher than the ACE recommendation.

Who is NLC?

National Learning Corporation (NLC) has been successfully preparing candidates for 40 years for over 5,000 exams. NLC publishes Passbook® study guides to help candidates prepare for all DANTES and CLEP exams and almost every other type of exam from high school through adult career.

Go to our website — www.passbooks.com — or call (800) 632-8888 for information about ordering our Passbooks.

To get detailed information on the DSST program and DSST preparation materials, visit www.getcollegecredit.com.

If you are interested in taking the DSST exams, call 877-471-9860 or e-mail pnj-dsst@thomson.com.

HISTORY OF THE SOVIET UNION
(Formerly, The Rise and Fall of the Soviet Union)

EXAM INFORMATION

This exam was developed to enable schools to award credit to students for knowledge equivalent to that learned by students taking the course. This exam covers Russia under the old regime, the revolutionary period, new economic policy, pre-war Stalinism, World War II, post-war Stalinism, the Khrushchev years, the Brezhnev era, and reform and collapse. (Formerly, Rise and Fall of the Soviet Union)

The exam contains 100 questions to be answered in 2 hours.

CREDIT RECOMMENDATIONS

The American Council on Education's College Credit Recommendation Service (ACE CREDIT) has evaluated the DSST test development process and content of this exam. It has made the following recommendations:

Area or Course Equivalent: History of the Soviet Union
Level: Upper-level baccalaureate
Amount of Credit: 3 Semester Hours
Minimum Score: 400

EXAM CONTENT OUTLINE

The following is an outline of the content areas covered in the examination. The approximate percentage of the examination devoted to each content area is also noted.

I. Russia Under the Old Regime – 10%
   a. Governing institutions
   b. Economics
   c. Culture and society
   d. Foreign Affairs
   e. Revolutionary movements

II. The Revolutionary Period 1914-1921 – 12%
   a. The first world war
   b. February/March revolution
   c. Interim
   d. Bolshevik revolution
   e. Civil war
   f. New Economic Policy (NEP)

III. Pre-War Stalinism – 13%
   a. Collectivization
   b. Industrialization
   c. Reign of terror
   d. Culture
   e. Nationalities

IV. The Second World War – 14%
   a. Pre-war foreign relations
   b. The course of the war
   c. The impact of the war
   d. Settlements of WWII and the origins of the Cold War

V. Postwar Stalinism – 11%

a. Reconstruction
   b. Nationalism
   c. Arms Race
   d. Cold War in Europe
   e. Cold War in Asia

VI. **The Khrushchev Years – 10%**
   a. Succession struggle
   b. De-Stalinization
   c. Soviet Relations with U.S under Khrushchev
   d. Rift with China
   e. Proxy Wars

VII. **The Brezhnev – 10%**
   a. Growth and stagnation
   b. Ideological dissent
   c. Detente
   d. Proxy wars in the Third World
   e. War in Afghanistan

VIII. **Reform and Collapse – 20%**
   a. Global Challengers (Thatcher, Reagan, Pope John Paul II)
   b. External factors (Afghanistan, Islam)
   c. Perestroika and glasnost
   d. Reemergence of the nationalities issue
   e. Revolutions in eastern Europe
   f. End of the Union of Soviet Socialist Republics
   g. Gorbachev's legacy

REFERENCES

Below is a list of reference publications that were either used as a reference to create the exam, or were used as textbooks in college courses of the same or similar title at the time the test was developed. You may reference either the current edition of these titles or textbooks currently used at a local college or university for the same class title. It is recommended that you reference more than one textbook on the topics outlined in this fact sheet.

You should begin by checking textbook content against the content outline provided before selecting textbooks that cover the test content from which to study.

Sources for study material are suggested but not limited to the following:

1. *The Rise and Fall of the Soviet Union,* McCauley, Martin, 1st edition, 20017. New York, NY: Longman.

2. *A concise History of Russia,* Bushkovitch, Paul. Cambridge: Cambridge University Press, Current Edition.

3. *The Soviet Experiment: Russia, the USSR, and the Successor States,* Suny, Ronald. Oxford: Oxford University Press, Current Edition.

SAMPLE QUESTIONS

All test questions are in a multiple-choice format, with one correct answer and three incorrect options. The following are samples of the types of questions that may appear on the exam.

1. The name of the lower house of the Russian parliament from 1906-1917 was?
   a. Council of State

    b. Council of the Federation
    c. State Duma
    d. Congress of People's Deputies

2. In his "April Theses" V.I. Lenin called for?
    a. support of the Russian war effort
    b. the overthrow of the provisional government
    c. cooperation with the Mensheviks
    d. peace with Germany

3. The Kornilov Affair hastened the October/ November Revolution by?
    a. strengthening the power of the army
    b. discrediting the constituent assembly
    c. increasing the popularity of Prime Minister Kerensky
    d. enhancing the prestige of the Bolsheviks

4. The purpose of Gosplan was to?
    a. coordinate secret surveillance of dissidents
    b. provide direction for economic development
    c. coordinate policies of the Orgburo and the Politburo
    d. train spies to infiltrate NATO

5. During the 1920's Soviet foreign policy enjoyed its greatest success in relations with?
    a. China
    b. Germany
    c. Great Britain
    d. The United States

6. Stalin's Industrial Five Year Plan of 1928 did which of the following?
    a. discouraged foreign investment.
    b. continued the policy of Lenin's NEP.
    c. built factories that produced heavy equipment.
    d. made the Soviet Union competitive with the west

7. The Katyn Forest Massacre created hostility toward the Soviet government among?
    a. Jews
    b. Finns
    c. Ukrainians
    d. Poles

8. In which of the following countries did communism come to power after the Second World War without Soviet assistance?
    a. Yugoslavia
    b. Poland
    c. Hungary
    d. Czechoslovakia

9. In June 1957, Khrushchev deftly outflanked Malenkov, Molotov, Kaganovich, and Shepilov in the Central Committee of the CPSU; stigmatizing them as [the]?
    a. Gang of Four
    b. Anti-Party Group
    c. Anti-Leninist Faction
    d. Neo-Stalinists

10. Which of the following was **NOT** a major economic trend of the Era of Stagnation?
    a. growth in the quantity of production

    b. success in "showcase industries" such as aerospace
    c. widespread shortages of consumer goods
    d. penetration of world markets by cheap Soviet exports

11. The nationality of the Soviet foreign minister during most of the Gorbachev era was?
    a. Russian
    b. Ukrainian
    c. Georgian
    d. Armenian

12. The catalyst for the aborted coup of August 1991 was Gorbachev's attempt to?
    a. dissolve collective farms
    b. remove from the constitution the article on the communist party's "leading role"
    c. reconstruct the federal union
    d. dissolve the congress of people's deputies

Answers to sample questions:
1-C, 2-B, 3-D, 4-B, 5-B, 6-C, 7-D, 8-A, 9-B, 10-D, 11-C, 12-C

HOW TO TAKE A TEST

You have studied long, hard and conscientiously.

With your official admission card in hand, and your heart pounding, you have been admitted to the examination room.

You note that there are several hundred other applicants in the examination room waiting to take the same test.

They all appear to be equally well prepared.

You know that nothing but your best effort will suffice. The "moment of truth" is at hand: you now have to demonstrate objectively, in writing, your knowledge of content and your understanding of subject matter.

You are fighting the most important battle of your life—to pass and/or score high on an examination which will determine your career and provide the economic basis for your livelihood.

What extra, special things should you know and should you do in taking the examination?

I. YOU MUST PASS AN EXAMINATION

A. WHAT EVERY CANDIDATE SHOULD KNOW
    Examination applicants often ask us for help in preparing for the written test. What can I study in advance? What kinds of questions will be asked? How will the test be given? How will the papers be graded?

B. HOW ARE EXAMS DEVELOPED?
    Examinations are carefully written by trained technicians who are specialists in the field known as "psychological measurement," in consultation with recognized authorities in the field of work that the test will cover. These experts recommend the subject matter areas or skills to be tested; only those knowledges or skills important to your success on the job are included. The most reliable books and source materials available are used as references. Together, the experts and technicians judge the difficulty level of the questions.
    Test technicians know how to phrase questions so that the problem is clearly stated. Their ethics do not permit "trick" or "catch" questions. Questions may have been tried out on sample groups, or subjected to statistical analysis, to determine their usefulness.
    Written tests are often used in combination with performance tests, ratings of training and experience, and oral interviews. All of these measures combine to form the best-known means of finding the right person for the right job.

II. HOW TO PASS THE WRITTEN TEST

A. BASIC STEPS

1) Study the announcement

How, then, can you know what subjects to study? Our best answer is: "Learn as much as possible about the class of positions for which you've applied." The exam will test the knowledge, skills and abilities needed to do the work.

Your most valuable source of information about the position you want is the official exam announcement. This announcement lists the training and experience qualifications. Check these standards and apply only if you come reasonably close to meeting them. Many jurisdictions preview the written test in the exam announcement by including a section called "Knowledge and Abilities Required," "Scope of the Examination," or some similar heading. Here you will find out specifically what fields will be tested.

2) Choose appropriate study materials

If the position for which you are applying is technical or advanced, you will read more advanced, specialized material. If you are already familiar with the basic principles of your field, elementary textbooks would waste your time. Concentrate on advanced textbooks and technical periodicals. Think through the concepts and review difficult problems in your field.

These are all general sources. You can get more ideas on your own initiative, following these leads. For example, training manuals and publications of the government agency which employs workers in your field can be useful, particularly for technical and professional positions. A letter or visit to the government department involved may result in more specific study suggestions, and certainly will provide you with a more definite idea of the exact nature of the position you are seeking.

3) Study this book!

III. KINDS OF TESTS

Tests are used for purposes other than measuring knowledge and ability to perform specified duties. For some positions, it is equally important to test ability to make adjustments to new situations or to profit from training. In others, basic mental abilities not dependent on information are essential. Questions which test these things may not appear as pertinent to the duties of the position as those which test for knowledge and information. Yet they are often highly important parts of a fair examination. For very general questions, it is almost impossible to help you direct your study efforts. What we can do is to point out some of the more common of these general abilities needed in public service positions and describe some typical questions.

1) General information

Broad, general information has been found useful for predicting job success in some kinds of work. This is tested in a variety of ways, from vocabulary lists to questions about current events. Basic background in some field of work, such as sociology or economics, may be sampled in a group of questions. Often these are principles which have become familiar to most persons through exposure rather than through formal training. It is difficult to advise you how to study for these questions; being alert to the world around you is our best suggestion.

2) Verbal ability

An example of an ability needed in many positions is verbal or language ability. Verbal ability is, in brief, the ability to use and understand words. Vocabulary and grammar tests are typical measures of this ability. Reading comprehension or paragraph interpretation questions are common in many kinds of civil service tests. You are given a paragraph of written material and asked to find its central meaning.

IV. KINDS OF QUESTIONS

1. Multiple-choice Questions

Most popular of the short-answer questions is the "multiple choice" or "best answer" question. It can be used, for example, to test for factual knowledge, ability to solve problems or judgment in meeting situations found at work.

A multiple-choice question is normally one of three types:
- It can begin with an incomplete statement followed by several possible endings. You are to find the one ending which best completes the statement, although some of the others may not be entirely wrong.
- It can also be a complete statement in the form of a question which is answered by choosing one of the statements listed.
- It can be in the form of a problem – again you select the best answer.

Here is an example of a multiple-choice question with a discussion which should give you some clues as to the method for choosing the right answer:

When an employee has a complaint about his assignment, the action which will best help him overcome his difficulty is to
  A. discuss his difficulty with his coworkers
  B. take the problem to the head of the organization
  C. take the problem to the person who gave him the assignment
  D. say nothing to anyone about his complaint

In answering this question, you should study each of the choices to find which is best. Consider choice "A" – Certainly an employee may discuss his complaint with fellow employees, but no change or improvement can result, and the complaint remains unresolved. Choice "B" is a poor choice since the head of the organization probably does not know what assignment you have been given, and taking your problem to him is known as "going over the head" of the supervisor. The supervisor, or person who made the assignment, is the person who can clarify it or correct any injustice. Choice "C" is, therefore, correct. To say nothing, as in choice "D," is unwise. Supervisors have and interest in knowing the problems employees are facing, and the employee is seeking a solution to his problem.

2. True/False

3. Matching Questions

Matching an answer from a column of choices within another column.

V. RECORDING YOUR ANSWERS

Computer terminals are used more and more today for many different kinds of exams.

For an examination with very few applicants, you may be told to record your answers in the test booklet itself. Separate answer sheets are much more common. If this separate answer sheet is to be scored by machine – and this is often the case – it is highly important that you mark your answers correctly in order to get credit.

VI. BEFORE THE TEST

YOUR PHYSICAL CONDITION IS IMPORTANT

If you are not well, you can't do your best work on tests. If you are half asleep, you can't do your best either. Here are some tips:

1) Get about the same amount of sleep you usually get. Don't stay up all night before the test, either partying or worrying—DON'T DO IT!
2) If you wear glasses, be sure to wear them when you go to take the test. This goes for hearing aids, too.
3) If you have any physical problems that may keep you from doing your best, be sure to tell the person giving the test. If you are sick or in poor health, you relay cannot do your best on any test. You can always come back and take the test some other time.

Common sense will help you find procedures to follow to get ready for an examination. Too many of us, however, overlook these sensible measures. Indeed, nervousness and fatigue have been found to be the most serious reasons why applicants fail to do their best on civil service tests. Here is a list of reminders:

- Begin your preparation early – Don't wait until the last minute to go scurrying around for books and materials or to find out what the position is all about.
- Prepare continuously – An hour a night for a week is better than an all-night cram session. This has been definitely established. What is more, a night a week for a month will return better dividends than crowding your study into a shorter period of time.
- Locate the place of the exam – You have been sent a notice telling you when and where to report for the examination. If the location is in a different town or otherwise unfamiliar to you, it would be well to inquire the best route and learn something about the building.
- Relax the night before the test – Allow your mind to rest. Do not study at all that night. Plan some mild recreation or diversion; then go to bed early and get a good night's sleep.
- Get up early enough to make a leisurely trip to the place for the test – This way unforeseen events, traffic snarls, unfamiliar buildings, etc. will not upset you.
- Dress comfortably – A written test is not a fashion show. You will be known by number and not by name, so wear something comfortable.
- Leave excess paraphernalia at home – Shopping bags and odd bundles will get in your way. You need bring only the items mentioned in the official notice you received; usually everything you need is provided. Do not bring reference books to the exam. They will only confuse those last minutes and be taken away from you when in the test room.

- Arrive somewhat ahead of time – If because of transportation schedules you must get there very early, bring a newspaper or magazine to take your mind off yourself while waiting.
- Locate the examination room – When you have found the proper room, you will be directed to the seat or part of the room where you will sit. Sometimes you are given a sheet of instructions to read while you are waiting. Do not fill out any forms until you are told to do so; just read them and be prepared.
- Relax and prepare to listen to the instructions
- If you have any physical problem that may keep you from doing your best, be sure to tell the test administrator. If you are sick or in poor health, you really cannot do your best on the exam. You can come back and take the test some other time.

VII. AT THE TEST

The day of the test is here and you have the test booklet in your hand. The temptation to get going is very strong. Caution! There is more to success than knowing the right answers. You must know how to identify your papers and understand variations in the type of short-answer question used in this particular examination. Follow these suggestions for maximum results from your efforts:

1) Cooperate with the monitor

The test administrator has a duty to create a situation in which you can be as much at ease as possible. He will give instructions, tell you when to begin, check to see that you are marking your answer sheet correctly, and so on. He is not there to guard you, although he will see that your competitors do not take unfair advantage. He wants to help you do your best.

2) Listen to all instructions

Don't jump the gun! Wait until you understand all directions. In most civil service tests you get more time than you need to answer the questions. So don't be in a hurry. Read each word of instructions until you clearly understand the meaning. Study the examples, listen to all announcements and follow directions. Ask questions if you do not understand what to do.

3) Identify your papers

Civil service exams are usually identified by number only. You will be assigned a number; you must not put your name on your test papers. Be sure to copy your number correctly. Since more than one exam may be given, copy your exact examination title.

4) Plan your time

Unless you are told that a test is a "speed" or "rate of work" test, speed itself is usually not important. Time enough to answer all the questions will be provided, but this does not mean that you have all day. An overall time limit has been set. Divide the total time (in minutes) by the number of questions to determine the approximate time you have for each question.

5) Do not linger over difficult questions

If you come across a difficult question, mark it with a paper clip (useful to have along) and come back to it when you have been through the booklet. One caution if you do this – be sure to skip a number on your answer sheet as well. Check often to be sure that you have not lost your place and that you are marking in the row numbered the same as the question you are answering.

6) Read the questions

Be sure you know what the question asks! Many capable people are unsuccessful because they failed to read the questions correctly.

7) Answer all questions

Unless you have been instructed that a penalty will be deducted for incorrect answers, it is better to guess than to omit a question.

8) Speed tests

It is often better NOT to guess on speed tests. It has been found that on timed tests people are tempted to spend the last few seconds before time is called in marking answers at random – without even reading them – in the hope of picking up a few extra points. To discourage this practice, the instructions may warn you that your score will be "corrected" for guessing. That is, a penalty will be applied. The incorrect answers will be deducted from the correct ones, or some other penalty formula will be used.

9) Review your answers

If you finish before time is called, go back to the questions you guessed or omitted to give them further thought. Review other answers if you have time.

10) Return your test materials

If you are ready to leave before others have finished or time is called, take ALL your materials to the monitor and leave quietly. Never take any test material with you. The monitor can discover whose papers are not complete, and taking a test booklet may be grounds for disqualification.

VIII. EXAMINATION TECHNIQUES

1) Read the general instructions carefully. These are usually printed on the first page of the exam booklet. As a rule, these instructions refer to the timing of the examination; the fact that you should not start work until the signal and must stop work at a signal, etc. If there are any special instructions, such as a choice of questions to be answered, make sure that you note this instruction carefully.

2) When you are ready to start work on the examination, that is as soon as the signal has been given, read the instructions to each question booklet, underline any key words or phrases, such as least, best, outline, describe and the like. In this way you will tend to answer as requested rather than discover on reviewing your paper that you listed without describing, that you selected the worst choice rather than the best choice, etc.

3) If the examination is of the objective or multiple-choice type – that is, each question will also give a series of possible answers: A, B, C or D, and you are called upon to select the best answer and write the letter next to that answer on your answer paper – it is advisable to start answering each question in turn. There may be anywhere from 50 to 100 such questions in the three or four hours allotted and you can see how much time would be taken if you read through all the questions before beginning to answer any. Furthermore, if you

come across a question or group of questions which you know would be difficult to answer, it would undoubtedly affect your handling of all the other questions.

4) If the examination is of the essay type and contains but a few questions, it is a moot point as to whether you should read all the questions before starting to answer any one. Of course, if you are given a choice – say five out of seven and the like – then it is essential to read all the questions so you can eliminate the two that are most difficult. If, however, you are asked to answer all the questions, there may be danger in trying to answer the easiest one first because you may find that you will spend too much time on it. The best technique is to answer the first question, then proceed to the second, etc.

5) Time your answers. Before the exam begins, write down the time it started, then add the time allowed for the examination and write down the time it must be completed, then divide the time available somewhat as follows:
    - If 3-1/2 hours are allowed, that would be 210 minutes. If you have 80 objective-type questions, that would be an average of 2-1/2 minutes per question. Allow yourself no more than 2 minutes per question, or a total of 160 minutes, which will permit about 50 minutes to review.
    - If for the time allotment of 210 minutes there are 7 essay questions to answer, that would average about 30 minutes a question. Give yourself only 25 minutes per question so that you have about 35 minutes to review.

6) The most important instruction is to read each question and make sure you know what is wanted. The second most important instruction is to time yourself properly so that you answer every question. The third most important instruction is to answer every question. Guess if you have to but include something for each question. Remember that you will receive no credit for a blank and will probably receive some credit if you write something in answer to an essay question. If you guess a letter – say "B" for a multiple-choice question – you may have guessed right. If you leave a blank as an answer to a multiple-choice question, the examiners may respect your feelings but it will not add a point to your score. Some exams may penalize you for wrong answers, so in such cases only, you may not want to guess unless you have some basis for your answer.

7) Suggestions
    a. Objective-type questions
        1. Examine the question booklet for proper sequence of pages and questions
        2. Read all instructions carefully
        3. Skip any question which seems too difficult; return to it after all other questions have been answered
        4. Apportion your time properly; do not spend too much time on any single question or group of questions
        5. Note and underline key words – all, most, fewest, least, best, worst, same, opposite, etc.
        6. Pay particular attention to negatives
        7. Note unusual option, e.g., unduly long, short, complex, different or similar in content to the body of the question
        8. Observe the use of "hedging" words – probably, may, most likely, etc.

9. Make sure that your answer is put next to the same number as the question
10. Do not second-guess unless you have good reason to believe the second answer is definitely more correct
11. Cross out original answer if you decide another answer is more accurate; do not erase until you are ready to hand your paper in
12. Answer all questions; guess unless instructed otherwise
13. Leave time for review

b. Essay questions
   1. Read each question carefully
   2. Determine exactly what is wanted. Underline key words or phrases.
   3. Decide on outline or paragraph answer
   4. Include many different points and elements unless asked to develop any one or two points or elements
   5. Show impartiality by giving pros and cons unless directed to select one side only
   6. Make and write down any assumptions you find necessary to answer the questions
   7. Watch your English, grammar, punctuation and choice of words
   8. Time your answers; don't crowd material

8) Answering the essay question

Most essay questions can be answered by framing the specific response around several key words or ideas. Here are a few such key words or ideas:

M's: manpower, materials, methods, money, management
P's: purpose, program, policy, plan, procedure, practice, problems, pitfalls, personnel, public relations

a. Six basic steps in handling problems:
   1. Preliminary plan and background development
   2. Collect information, data and facts
   3. Analyze and interpret information, data and facts
   4. Analyze and develop solutions as well as make recommendations
   5. Prepare report and sell recommendations
   6. Install recommendations and follow up effectiveness

b. Pitfalls to avoid
1. Taking things for granted – A statement of the situation does not necessarily imply that each of the elements is necessarily true; for example, a complaint may be invalid and biased so that all that can be taken for granted is that a complaint has been registered
2. Considering only one side of a situation – Wherever possible, indicate several alternatives and then point out the reasons you selected the best one
3. Failing to indicate follow up – Whenever your answer indicates action on your part, make certain that you will take proper follow-up action to see how successful your recommendations, procedures or actions turn out to be
4. Taking too long in answering any single question – Remember to time your answers properly

EXAMINATION SECTION

EXAMINATION SECTION
TEST 1

DIRECTIONS: Each question or incomplete statement is followed by several suggested answers or completions. Select the one that BEST answers the question or completes the statement. *PRINT THE LETTER OF THE CORRECT ANSWER IN THE SPACE AT THE RIGHT.*

1. Which of the following was NOT a distinct state region of the Soviet Union?

    A. Transcaucasus
    B. Baltic
    C. Central Asian
    D. Siberian

    1.____

2. Leonid Brezhnev looked forward to signing the Helsinki Accords in 1975 mostly because the treaty

    A. would give Western nations the impression that the Soviet Union was ready to recognize the civil rights of Soviet citizens
    B. would officially consolidate the territorial gains the Soviet Union had made during the post-war era
    C. would grant important civil rights, such as freedom of speech and freedom of religion, to Soviet citizens
    D. assured that the United States would not use force against any nation that had not attacked it first

    2.____

3. When the Soviet Union was initially established, it consisted of _____ republics.

    A. 4
    B. 8
    C. 11
    D. 15

    3.____

4. The rise of the Russian monarchy was, to a significant degree, a response to the external threat posed by the

    A. Mongol Khans
    B. Prussian monarchy
    C. English crown
    D. Japanese empire

    4.____

5. The 1972 SALT I Treaty placed NO limitations on the number of

    A. intercontinental ballistic missiles (ICBMs)
    B. warheads, or multiple independently targetable reentry vehicles (MIRVs)
    C. submarine-launched ballistic missiles (SLBMs)
    D. anti-ballistic missiles (ABMs)

    5.____

6. Boris Yeltsins' "shock therapy" was based on each of the following, EXCEPT

    A. devaluation of the ruble
    B. opening the economy to international influences
    C. privatization of most state-owned enterprises

    6.____

D. ending price controls

7. The Congress of People's Deputies, as re-created by Gorbachev, provided Soviet citizens with each of the following, EXCEPT

   A. an end to communist ideology in government
   B. free elections
   C. the introduction of reform candidates
   D. the defeat of same major party figures

7._____

8. Lenin believed that imperialism was
   I. a phase of capitalism in which all the earth's territories would be divided among the great capitalist powers
   II. the first phase in the spread of capitalism
   III. a phase in which monopolies and finance capitalists come to dominate
   IV. a phase of capitalism in which the export of capital has acquired a chief importance

   A. I and II
   B. I, III and IV
   C. II and IV
   D. I, II, III and IV

8._____

9. After World War II, the Catholic Church remained an influential force in the Soviet-dominated country of

   A. Czechoslovakia
   B. Romania
   C. Hungary
   D. Poland

9._____

10. At the beginning of the twentieth century, about _____ out of every 10 Russians was a peasant who had few political rights.

    A. 7
    B. 5
    C. 7
    D. 9

10._____

11. Which of the following was NOT a problem for Soviet economic planning after Stalin's death?

    A. Managers often exceeded their production goals and skewed the entire system.
    B. The cost of capital was not effectively anticipated or accommodated.
    C. There were few incentives to facilitate technological advances.
    D. Quantity was emphasized over quality.

11._____

12. The nationalist party that emerged after the collapse of the Soviet Union was the

    A. Liberal Democratic Party of Russia
    B. Fair Russia Party
    C. United Russia Party
    D. Communist Party of the Russian Federation

12._____

13. Of the following Bolsheviks, which was the first to be executed during the Great Purge of the late 1930s?   13._____

    A. Rykov
    B. Zinoviev
    C. Bukharin
    D. Tukhachevsky

14. During the early Soviet era, one strategy used to achieve cultural unification was the   14._____

    A. prohibition against active Islamic worship
    B. resettlement of ethnic Russians throughout the peripheral republics to provide skilled labor
    C. endowment of the Russian Orthodox Church to extend its ministries to outer republics, especially those where Islam was practiced
    D. promotion of non-Russian languages in government administration, the courts, the schools, and the mass media

15. In what year did Gorbachev discard the Brezhnev Doctrine?   15._____

    A. 1986
    B. 1988
    C. 1990
    D. 1992

16. Russia's conquest of Central Asia during the 19th century was driven by   16._____
    I. the need for more land to accommodate a growing population
    II. a desire for ports on the Indian Ocean
    III. Russian nationalism
    IV. a desire for the region's natural resources

    A. I and II
    B. I and III
    C. II, III and IV
    D. I, II, III and IV

17. In post-soviet Russia, each of the following issues served as a political wedge that divided the Russian people, EXCEPT   17._____

    A. Westernization
    B. religion
    C. the economy
    D. national identity

18. The key year of the Russian Civil War, in which the White Armies were roundly defeated in the south and the Caucasus, was   18._____

    A. 1917
    B. 1919
    C. 1920
    D. 1921

19. Following the Russian Revolution, the Bolsheviks appeared to introduce a hierarchy within their "classless" system, with _____ occupying the top level.

    A. Government officials
    B. Industrial laborers
    C. The intelligentsia
    D. Rural peasants

19._____

20. In 1967, the Soviet Union signed a treaty with the United States and Britain that banned the

    A. placement of nuclear weapons in any unstable Third World country
    B. development of an anti-missile defense system
    C. placement of nuclear weapons in orbit around the earth, or on the moon
    D. use of nuclear weapons in any manner other than defensive

20._____

21. The main reason for the Bolsheviks' execution of the tsar and his family was

    A. to create a power vacuum that could be filled by Lenin
    B. for revenge
    C. as punishment for their crimes against Russia
    D. to prevent approaching enemy soldiers from capturing the town and freeing him

21._____

22. The primary religion among the Soviet Union's Central Asian states was

    A. Russian Orthodox
    B. Islam
    C. Eastern Orthodox
    D. There was no religion, as religious observance was banned by the Communist Party.

22._____

23. The Kronstadt rebellion was staged by

    A. German-planted agitators posing as Russian workers
    B. peasants whose land had been seized
    C. Soviet sailors
    D. wealthy farmers

23._____

24. Following World War II, the Soviet model of industrialization and central planning was spread to other parts of the world primarily through

    A. military brute force
    B. the reforms of local leaders
    C. subterfuge and espionage
    D. an exhaustive program of communist indoctrination

24._____

25. Which of the following was ceded to Russia by Sweden in the 1809 Treaty of Fredrikshamn?

    A. Norway
    B. Latvia
    C. Lithuania
    D. Finland

25._____

26. The Triple Alliance, formed in 1882, lasted until 1914. Which of the following was NOT a member of the Triple Alliance?

    A. Austria-Hungary
    B. Germany
    C. Italy
    D. Ottoman Empire

26._____

27. Which Soviet leader renewed the government's persecutions of the Russian Orthodox Church and promised to show the "last priest" on Soviet television?

    A. Stalin
    B. Khrushchev
    C. Brezhnev
    D. Andropov

27._____

28. After World War II, Stalin

    A. relaxed Soviet control of some Eastern European nations
    B. permitted cultural freedom while insisting on political submission
    C. revived forced-labor camps
    D. permitted Soviets who lived abroad to remain in political asylum

28._____

29. Which of the following was NOT an essential characteristic of the Soviet Union's successful defense of Nazi aggression during World War II?

    A. Widespread Russian outrage at the German treatment of Jews in Eastern Europe
    B. The Soviets' prodigious industrial capacity
    C. Soviet counterattacks during the coldest parts of winter
    D. The great manpower reserves of the Soviets

29._____

30. The last attempt at a unified anti-Bolshevik government, the Provisional All-Russian Government, was headquartered in _____ during the Russian Civil War.

    A. Moscow
    B. Omsk
    C. Kiev
    D. St. Petersburg

30._____

31. The most significant problems in Eastern Europe and Russia in the post-Soviet era have generally involved

    A. an unwillingness by Western nations to lend advice
    B. poorly educated populations
    C. an uneven shift from central economic planning to a market economy
    D. the refusal of government leaders to allow foreign investment.

31._____

32. During the 1930s, Soviet production in each of the following sectors dropped precipitously, EXCEPT

    A. steel
    B. agriculture
    C. coal
    D. chemicals

32._____

33. At the 1878 Congress of Berlin, Russia gained the territories of
    I. Bessarabia
    II. Kars in Armenia
    III. Dobruja
    IV. Eastern Rumelia

    A. I and II
    B. II only
    C. II and III
    D. I, II, III and IV

34. Imre Nagy was the politician who attempted to liberalize the nation of _____ and withdraw it from the Warsaw Pact.

    A. Czechoslovakia
    B. Romania
    C. Yugoslavia
    D. Hungary

35. The United States officially recognized the Soviet regime in

    A. 1928
    B. 1933
    C. 1954
    D. 1982

36. After the Russian Revolution, which of the following moderates wanted to restrict the reforms to a parliamentary democracy?

    A. Prince Georgii Lvov
    B. Alexander Kerensky
    C. Alexander Kolchak
    D. Josef Stalin

37. Which of the following, known as the "father of Russian socialism," is credited with creating the political climate that enabled the emancipation of the serfs?

    A. Frederich Engels
    B. Alexander Herzen
    C. Sergei Witte
    D. Karl Marx

38. The Socialist-Revolutionary Party's platform's main difference with that of the Social Democratic Party was the that the Socialist-Revolutionary Party

    A. advocated a large party of activists with broad representation
    B. was not Marxist
    C. supported universal suffrage
    D. believed the industrial proletariat would be the revolutionary class

39. Shortly after Khrushchev announced the policy of de-Stalinization, a revolt broke out in   39.____
    I. Hungary
    II. Poland
    III. Tblisi
    IV. Yugoslavia

    A. I and II
    B. I, II and IV
    C. III only
    D. I, II, III and IV

40. Typically, the first to be brought to trial during the purges of the Stalin regime were   40.____

    A. peasants
    B. low-level office-holders
    C. high officials and leaders of the Bolshevik revolution
    D. political dissidents

KEY (CORRECT ANSWERS)

1. D	11. A	21. D	31. C
2. B	12. A	22. B	32. B
3. A	13. B	23. C	33. A
4. A	14. D	24. A	34. D
5. B	15. A	25. D	35. B
6. A	16. C	26. D	36. A
7. A	17. B	27. B	37. B
8. B	18. B	28. C	38. B
9. D	19. A	29. A	39. A
10. D	20. C	30. B	40. C

TEST 2

DIRECTIONS: Each question or incomplete statement is followed by several suggested answers or completions. Select the one that BEST answers the question or completes the statement. *PRINT THE LETTER OF THE CORRECT ANSWER IN THE SPACE AT THE RIGHT.*

1. The First Balkan War, in 1912, was settled on terms that resulted in the creation of the independent state of

    A. Serbia
    B. Bulgaria
    C. Macedonia
    D. Albania

    1._____

2. The "Holodomor" refers to a widespread famine in 1932-1933 that killed between 3 million and 5 million people in the Soviet republic of

    A. Ukraine
    B. Belarus
    C. Moldova
    D. Chechnya

    2._____

3. Mikhail Gorbachev proved willing to do each of the following, EXCEPT

    A. terminate the arms race with the United States
    B. allow great autonomy for the Soviet republics
    C. invite capitalist investment in Russia
    D. end Russian control of Eastern Europe

    3._____

4. After the 1861 emancipation of the serfs, a revolutionary movement arose whose members were known as

    A. Bolsheviks
    B. Trudoviks
    C. Narodniks
    D. Mensheviks

    4._____

5. In 1939, the Soviet Union fought an undeclared border war with

    A. Japan
    B. India
    C. China
    D. Afghanistan

    5._____

6. The Battle of Poltava, fought in 1709, brought about
    I. the end of Sweden's role as a great power
    II. an independent Ukraine
    III. the rise of Imperial Russia
    IV. a gradual weakening of Prussia's hold on Eastern Europe

    A. I only
    B. I and III
    C. II and II

    6._____

8

D. I, II, III and IV

7. In Europe, throughout the 1980s, the communist ideology began to

   A. be viewed unfavorably in light of the economic successes of capitalist countries
   B. take hold in Western Europe as the Soviet economy gained strength
   C. enjoy a resurgence on the heels of the Green Party's successes
   D. become fashionable among an increasing number of young people

8. Under Catherine the Great, Russia annexed each of the following territories, EXCEPT

   A. Belarus
   B. the Baltic States
   C. Western Ukraine
   D. part of Poland

9. Which of the following was NOT one of the secret protocols of the Molotov-Ribbentrop Pact?

   A. western Poland would be ceded to Germany
   B. Bessarabia would be ceded to the Soviet Union
   C. Lithuania would be ceded to the Soviet Union
   D. Finland would be ceded to the Soviet Union

10. Stalin's territorial ambitions after World War II could best be described as

    A. a tool for realizing world revolution
    B. directed at the centers of least resistance in Africa and Asia
    C. limited to regaining the territories lost to Germany after World War I
    D. aimed at the Americas, to pose a more direct threat to the United States

11. From the 1930s to the 1950s, the Soviet economic strategy shifted capacity from

    A. durable goods to non-durable goods
    B. consumer goods to producer goods
    C. capital goods to luxury goods
    D. producer goods to consumer goods

12. The "Khrushchev Thaw" refers to a period in Soviet history when

    A. domestic repression and censorship reached a low point
    B. Brezhnev began to gain power within the Communist Party apparatus
    C. Communist Party elites began to warm to Khrushchev's policy recommendations
    D. the country escalated its production of nuclear weapons

13. Which of the following was NOT a foreign policy change implemented by Mikhail Gorbachev?

    A. Satellite autonomy programs
    B. Disarmament programs
    C. Greater control of satellite nations
    D. Defense spending reductions

14. In reality, Nicholas II's October Manifesto

   A. did not result in a significant increase in freedom of government representation for most Russians
   B. raised Lenin's profile among the revolutionary movement
   C. united the two main revolutionary factions within Russia
   D. weakened the tsar's hold on power enough that he was never able to regain it

15. The tsar who finally rescued Russia from the Mongols was

   A. Fyodor I
   B. Ivan I
   C. Boris Godunov
   D. Ivan IV ("Ivan the Terrible")

16. By 1900, the expansion of the Russian Empire had begun to focus on the region of

   A. Northeast Asia
   B. Southeast Asia
   C. The Transcaucasus
   D. Scandinavia

17. Which of the following would LEAST likely have been on the side of the Whites during the Russian Civil War?

   A. Tsarist officials and military
   B. Political organizations that had been excluded from power
   C. Industrial workers
   D. Peasants upset at Lenin's crop seizures

18. During the Russian Civil War, the White Army carried out an offensive was aided by 40,000 troops from _____ that captured nearly 5000 miles of the Trans-Siberian Railroad and assumed control of several major towns.

   A. Great Britain
   B. Czechoslovakia
   C. Japan
   D. Canada

19. Shortly after the reunification of East and West Germany in 1990, the East German people

   A. fled in large numbers across the eastern border to Poland
   B. elected non-Communist leaders
   C. suffered from widespread ethnic unrest
   D. staged widespread protests

20. The abolition of serfdom in Imperial Russia resulted in
   I. a change in status and circumstances for about 52 million Russians
   II. the immediate emancipation of domestic serfs
   III. the establishment of village mirs that would collect taxes and make determinations about crops
   IV. serfs becoming owners of their own lands, but paying for it over time with interest

A. I and II
B. I, III and IV
C. II and IV
D. I, II, III and IV

21. The root cause of the Soviet Union's resentment for the Allies' conduct of World War II was

    A. the slowness with which the Allies opened a second European front
    B. Stalin's exclusion from the Casablanca Conference
    C. U.S. exclusion of the Soviet Union from the Lend-Lease Act
    D. U.S. refusal to have official contact with a communist regime

22. For about 40 years after World War II, Soviet-bloc nations generally

    A. achieved significant industrial growth, but lagged behind capitalist economies in consumer goods and technologies.
    B. surpassed capitalist countries in agricultural production and the manufacturing of consumer goods, but lagged behind in the development of military technology.
    C. were oligarchies that did not substantially improve the living standards of the general population
    D. failed to rebuild industries that had been damaged or destroyed in the war.

23. Khiva, Bukhara, and Kokand, three khanates that were colonized by the Russians in 1866-1876, are now mainly situated in the independent republic of

    A. Azerbaijan
    B. Uzbekistan
    C. Ukraine
    D. Kazakhstan

24. The Provisional Government's aim in replacing Prince Lvov with Alexander Kerensky was to

    A. find a leader who could extricate Russia from World War I
    B. take a harder line against the Bolsheviks
    C. force the exile of Leon Trotsky
    D. regain popularity with the people

25. In what year was the Soviet Union officially founded?

    A. 1918
    B. 1920
    C. 1922
    D. 1928

26. One important similarity between Lenin's New Economic Policy and Gorbachev's perestroika was that they both aimed to

    A. build a strong military through industrialization
    B. make the Soviet Union an essentially agrarian society
    C. increase production through individual resourcefulness
    D. tighten the controls of central planning

27. Stalinist society was characterized by

    A. discrimination of women in the work force
    B. the politicization of art, literature, and science
    C. the rise of the Russian Orthodox Church
    D. slow, measured economic and industrial growth

27.____

28. Russia's membership in the Triple Entente was essentially terminated by the

    A. Molotov-Ribbentrop pact
    B. German attack on Stalingrad
    C. the Treaty of Brest-Litovsk
    D. Battle of Port Arthur

28.____

29. The top priority for Stalin's Soviet economy was

    A. aid in reconstructing East Germany
    B. producing consumer goods
    C. improving the living standards of the nation's poor
    D. producing military goods

29.____

30. Which of the following was NOT a reform implemented by Tsar Alexander I?

    A. the adoption of a minimum-wage law
    B. establishing zemstvos to administer local governments
    C. establishing new rural and municipal police under the direction of the Ministry of the Interior
    D. the abolition of capital punishment

30.____

31. Which of the following nations formally withdrew from the Warsaw Pact in 1968 over ideological differences with the Soviet Union?

    A. Romania
    B. Czechoslovakia
    C. Yugoslavia
    D. Albania

31.____

32. Which of the following is considered to have been a major Soviet triumph over the United States during the Cold War?

    A. The Prague Spring
    B. The Cuban Missile Crisis
    C. The launch of Sputnik
    D. The response to the Hungarian rebellion

32.____

33. Yeltsin's radical market reforms resulted in each of the following, EXCEPT

    A. a severe depression
    B. widespread withdrawals of foreign investment in the Russian economy
    C. a decline in purchasing power for consumers
    D. a fifty-percent decrease in industrial production

33.____

34. In comparing Soviet politics to the politics of Communist China, it is clear that the Soviet Union

    A. used the Communist Party apparatus to exert greater control
    B. was more dramatically affected by divisions among ethnic and national groups
    C. was more accepting of the idea of women holding positions of high political authority
    D. used the army more effectively to exert control

35. The first attempts by counter-revolutionaries to regain power from the Bolsheviks were the _____ , in October of 1917.

    A. Kerensky-Krasnov uprising and the Junker mutiny
    B. Kornilov affair and Ice March
    C. Junker mutiny and Tambov rebellion
    D. The Cossack revolt and Kronstadt rebellion

36. The second largest republic of the Soviet Union, in terms of square mileage, was

    A. Ukraine
    B. Russia
    C. Uzbekistan
    D. Kazakhstan

37. During the Cold War, the Soviet Union was able to dominate the foreign policy of each of the following countries, EXCEPT

    A. Hungary
    B. Yugoslavia
    C. Czechoslovakia
    D. Bulgaria

38. Which of the following was a significant factor that brought about the end of detente?

    A. Brezhnev's and Ford's signing of the SALT II Treaty.
    B. The involvement of China in the Vietnam War
    C. The 1979 Soviet invasion of Afghanistan
    D. The 1978 fall of the Iranian Shah

39. The Soviet leader who today bears most of the blame for failing to make the transition to postindustrial society, unlike its Western rivals, is

    A. Stalin
    B. Brezhnev
    C. Khrushchev
    D. Andropov

40. During the Russian Civil War,
    I. The Reds relied on aid from secret allies, most significantly Germany
    II. Lenin used the Cheka to sniff out opposition to the Reds.
    III. several foreign powers, including the United States, intervened militarily against the Reds
    IV. the Whites were a unified group who wanted to make Russia into a democratic republic.

A. I and II
B. I, II and III
C. II and III
D. I, II, III and IV

KEY (CORRECT ANSWERS)

1.	D	11.	B	21.	A	31.	D
2.	A	12.	A	22.	A	32.	C
3.	B	13.	C	23.	B	33.	B
4.	C	14.	A	24.	D	34.	B
5.	A	15.	B	25.	C	35.	A
6.	B	16.	A	26.	C	36.	D
7.	A	17.	C	27.	B	37.	B
8.	B	18.	B	28.	C	38.	C
9.	C	19.	B	29.	D	39.	B
10.	C	20.	B	30.	A	40.	C

TEST 3

DIRECTIONS: Each question or incomplete statement is followed by several suggested answers or completions. Select the one that BEST answers the question or completes the statement. *PRINT THE LETTER OF THE CORRECT ANSWER IN THE SPACE AT THE RIGHT.*

1. The first Soviet atomic bomb, known in the U.S. as "Joe 1," was tested on August 29,   1.____

   A. 1946
   B. 1949
   C. 1951
   D. 1953

2. Khrushchev's "Secret Speech," delivered to the 20th Congress of the Communist Party in 1956, was titled   2.____

   A. History of the Fatherland
   B. On Permanent Revolution
   C. On the Personality Cult and Its Consequences
   D. About Our Revolution

3. The first major purge of the Communist Party ranks was performed in   3.____

   A. 1921 by the Bolsheviks
   B. 1932 by Stalin
   C. 1936 by Stalin
   D. 1942 by Stalin

4. The man who was proclaimed the "Supreme Ruler" of Russia in November of 1918 was   4.____

   A. Alexander Kolchak
   B. Leon Trotsky
   C. V. Lenin
   D. Prince Georgii Lvov

5. The tsar who is said to have founded Russia's navy is   5.____

   A. Boris Godunov
   B. Ivan IV
   C. Peter the Great
   D. Catherine the Great

6. Until about 1965, the foundation of Soviet economic development was   6.____

   A. balanced growth, with an emphasis on consumer goods
   B. a complex system of management incentives
   C. a very high ratio or investment to national income
   D. the agricultural sector

7. To what country did Bessarabia belong prior to 1940?   7.____

A. Jordan
B. Romania
C. Serbia
D. Turkey

8. Each of the following is widely considered to be a contributing cause of the Cold War, EXCEPT

   A. Russian suspicion of the United Nations
   B. Russian distrust of Allied strategy in World War II
   C. Soviet resentment over its exclusion from postwar politics in Western Europe
   D. disagreements over the interpretation of the Yalta pact

9. The most industrialized of the Soviet state regions was the

   A. Transcaucasus
   B. Baltic
   C. Central Asian
   D. Balkan

10. Provisions of Nicholas II's October Manifesto, issued in 1905, included
    I. a decree that no law should come into force without the con sent of the state Duma
    II. freedom of assembly
    III. universal suffrage for men and women
    IV. freedom of religion

    A. I only
    B. I, II and IV
    C. III and IV
    D. I, II, III and IV

11. Russian attempts to dominate the Balkans led to a war with _____ from 1828-1829.

    A. Greece
    B. Yugoslavia
    C. Turkey
    D. Austria-Hungary

12. The events that led to the regaining of independence for the Baltic States in the late 1980s were collectively termed the

    A. Baltic Spring
    B. Velvet Revolution
    C. Vilnius Movement
    D. Singing Revolution

13. Which of the following was NOT a member of the Warsaw Pact when it was established in 1955?

    A. Bulgaria
    B. Albania
    C. Yugoslavia
    D. East Germany

14. In the 1858 Treaty of Aigun, Russia gained _____ from China.

    A. the Amur region
    B. Kamchatka
    C. Manchuria
    D. Sakhalin Island

15. Internal unrest during the 1980s in the Soviet Union was due mostly to

    A. increasing competition for scarce natural resources
    B. increasing desires for ethnic autonomy
    C. the military's failure to implement new technology
    D. agricultural overproduction

16. Khrushchev's primary goal during the Berlin Crisis was to

    A. stop the flight of East Germans to West Berlin
    B. keep Western ideology from infiltrating East Berlin
    C. end East Germany's control over East Berlin
    D. bring West Germany into the Soviet sphere of influence

17. "Land, Peace, and Bread" was the slogan of

    A. the Bolsheviks
    B. Josef Stalin
    C. the Narodniks
    D. the White Russians

18. Which of the following was a reform introduced by Peter the Great?

    A. reducing the burdens of serfdom
    B. the creation of a Duma, or elected parliament
    C. eliminating the merit system in the state bureaucracy
    D. compulsory education for the upper classes

19. The end of communism was peaceful in each of the following Eastern European countries, EXCEPT

    A. Hungary
    B. Bulgaria
    C. Czechoslovakia
    D. Romania

20. Which of the following nations became a Soviet satellite after World War II?

    A. Lithuania
    B. Belarus
    C. Poland
    D. Ukraine

21. The revolutionary movement that arose in Russia after the emancipation of the serfs was composed primarily of

A. peasants and former serfs who wanted to overthrow the monarchy and distribute land among themselves
B. prosperous farmers who wanted to maintain the status quo and curtail the political influence of the newly freed serfs
C. industrial laborers who wanted to establish a socialist dictatorship by a soon-to-be-discovered Great Man
D. middle and upper class people who wanted to overthrow the monarchy and distribute land among the peasantry

22. Mao's regime in Communist China did not receive a significant amount of aid from the Soviet Union until after

A. Stalin had signed a neutrality pact with Japan
B. Mao hosted a visit by U.S. president Richard Nixon
C. China became involved in border conflict with India
D. the Mao regime had built up a sizeable army

23. Lenin's policy of War Communism was essentially

A. a plan to redistribute the nation's wealth
B. the application of the "total war" concept to a civil conflict
C. a plan to marshal the economic resources of Russia against the German enemy
D. a terror campaign carried out by the Cheka

24. Which of the following Soviet-bloc nations practiced a variation of communism called "consumer socialism," which introduced some market mechanisms, from 1962- 1973?

A. Czechoslovakia
B. Romania
C. Hungary
D. Yugoslavia

25. During the Cold war, ethnic disputes became a threat to the stability of each of the following Soviet-bloc nations, EXCEPT

A. Czechoslovakia
B. East Germany
C. Yugoslavia
D. Romania

26. Which of the following Balkan states was so militarily powerful that it was referred to as the "Prussia of the Balkans" in the early 20th century?

A. Serbia
B. Montenegro
C. Bulgaria
D. Bosnia

27. Gorbachev's economic reforms met their greatest resistance from

A. Communist Party and military leaders
B. Russian consumers who feared inflation
C. Boris Yeltsin
D. rural farmers

28. The 1881 assassination of Alexander II resulted in

    A. the liberation of Russian serfs
    B. a great setback for the reform movement in Russia
    C. the establishment of the Duma by his successor, Alexander III
    D. the execution of Lenin's brother, Alexander Ulyanov

29. Which of the following did NOT contribute to economic stagnation in Imperial Russia?

    A. Repressive domestic policies
    B. A dependence on imports
    C. The feudal agricultural system
    D. Russian territorial victories in the Crimean War

30. Which of the following events contributed to the forced retirement of Nikita Khrushchev?

    A. The Suez Crisis
    B. The establishment of the Warsaw Pact
    C. Rapprochement with Yugoslavia
    D. The Cuban Missile Crisis

31. The leader of the Prague Spring movement was

    A. Lech Walesa
    B. Vaclav Havel
    C. Andrei Sakharov
    D. Alexander Dubcek

32. Stalin's first Five-Year Plan was launched in

    A. 1925
    B. 1928
    C. 1932
    D. 1934

33. Which of the following was a secret police force of the Russian Empire?

    A. Imperial Duma
    B. Okhrana
    C. Cheka
    D. MVD

34. Which of the following was an important consequence of Gorbachev's reforms?

    A. Reawakened ethnic nationalism within the former Soviet Union
    B. An overall higher standard of living
    C. A resurgence of Russian influence in Eastern Europe
    D. Renewed support for the Communist Party

35. Of the following political parties, the _____ Party had NOT appeared in Russia by 1905.

    A. Socialist-Revolutionary
    B. Social Democratic Labor
    C. Christian Democratic
    D. Constitutional Democratic

36. Which of the following was NOT a member of the Triple Entente, formed in 1907?

    A. Russia
    B. Germany
    C. France
    D. Britain

37. In pre-Imperial Russia, boyars were

    A. peasant farmers
    B. regional administrators
    C. nominally servants, but essentially domestic slaves
    D. members of an elite aristocratic class

38. One of the strategies adopted by Vladimir Putin to counter the economic depression in Russia was to

    A. reform the pension system
    B. cut housing subsidies
    C. relax the conditions for trade union organization
    D. simplify the tax code

39. Lenin's theory of revolution was distinguished from that of Marx by Lenin's belief in the

    A. effectiveness of peasant guerilla warfare
    B. need for collectivized agriculture to follow a socialist revolution
    C. need for a highly centralized revolutionary vanguard to lead the people
    D. inevitability of socialist revolution

40. When the Petrograd Soviet issued Army Order No. 1 in 1917, its goal was to

    A. get rid of any officers who were loyal to the Provisional Government
    B. use the army as a police force to enforce martial law
    C. mobilize a Red Army for the coming civil war
    D. strengthen the army for the fight against the Central Powers in World War I

KEY (CORRECT ANSWERS)

1. B	11. C	21. D	31. D
2. C	12. D	22. A	32. B
3. A	13. C	23. B	33. B
4. A	14. A	24. C	34. A
5. C	15. B	25. B	35. C
6. C	16. A	26. C	36. B
7. B	17. A	27. A	37. D
8. A	18. D	28. B	38. C
9. B	19. D	29. D	39. C
10. B	20. C	30. D	40. A

TEST 4

DIRECTIONS: Each question or incomplete statement is followed by several suggested answers or completions. Select the one that BEST answers the question or completes the statement. *PRINT THE LETTER OF THE CORRECT ANSWER IN THE SPACE AT THE RIGHT.*

1. The upper house of the Russian parliament, established in 1993, is the   1.____

   A. Congress of People's Deputies
   B. State Duma
   C. Federal Assembly
   D. Federation Council of Russia

2. One of the most important nations to follow a policy of nonalignment during the Cold War was   2.____

   A. India
   B. Israel
   C. Taiwan
   D. Portugal

3. Gorbachev's reform policies included uskoreniye, meaning that the Soviet   3.____

   A. political system would be restructured
   B. economy would accelerate
   C. society would become more open
   D. economy would operate on market principles

4. Nihilism was a movement that developed in Russia during the   4.____

   A. 1860s
   B. 1880s
   C. 1920s
   D. 1950s

5. One result of the Treaty of Brest-Litovsk was that Russia   5.____

   A. lost about a third of its population, its most fertile and industrialized regions
   B. formed a non-aggression pact with Germany
   C. gained about a third more territory
   D. attempted to spread the revolution to Europe

6. In the Baltic States during the 1980s,   6.____
   I. the Estonian parliament declared its independence from the Soviet Union
   II. people staged massive protests against pollution created by Soviet industry
   III. there was a resurgence in nationalist movements that demanded autonomy
   IV. the Lithuanian parliament declared its independence from the Soviet Union

   A. I and II
   B. II and III
   C. II, III and IV
   D. I, II, III and IV

7. The Soviet leader who first implemented central economic planning was

   A. Nicholas II
   B. Lenin
   C. Bukharin
   D. Stalin

8. The Brezhnev era was a time when there was an unspoken social contract between the government and Soviet citizens. During the Brezhnev era, Russians were generally allowed each of the following, EXCEPT

   A. free social services
   B. the freedom to voice political dissent
   C. a measure of job security
   D. minimal interference in their personal lives

9. Which of the following did NOT fight as an enemy of Russia during the Crimean War?

   A. France
   B. Ottoman Empire
   C. Britain
   D. Austria-Hungary

10. Which of the following was NOT a factor that contributed to the onset of tensions between the Soviet Union and Communist China during the 1950s and 1960s?

    A. The Soviet Union's refusal to support China during a border dispute with India
    B. Soviet refusal to fulfill an earlier promise to provide China with nuclear weapons
    C. The Soviet Union's refusal to purchase Chinese goods
    D. Soviet provision of only modest aid to China

11. The _____ was the leading secret police organization of the Soviet Union during the Stalin regime.

    A. NKVD
    B. Okhrana
    C. Politburo
    D. Cheka

12. By 1990, _____ was the only Soviet-bloc state that was still unaffected by changes in Soviet policy.

    A. Romania
    B. East Germany
    C. Czechoslovakia
    D. Bulgaria

13. The moderate workers party that emerged in early 20th century Russia and won seats in the State Duma after the 1905 revolution, were the

    A. Bolsheviks
    B. Narodniks
    C. Mensheviks
    D. Trudoviks

14. Which of the following ethnic groups does NOT speak a Slavic language?

    A. Bosnians
    B. Czechs
    C. Magyars
    D. Serbs

15. It is generally agreed by historians today that the global limits of U.S. and Soviet influence were exposed during the

    A. 1950s
    B. 1960s
    C. 1970s
    D. 1980s

16. The last leader of the Russian Whites in the Civil War was

    A. Wrangel
    B. Denikin
    C. Kornilov
    D. Kolchak

17. The Council for Mutual Economic Assistance (COMECON) was organized in 1949 as a(n)

    A. attempt to integrate the markets of Eastern and Western Europe
    B. exclusive trade union to deny goods produced in communist countries from reaching capitalist markets
    C. espionage organization that operated under the cover of economic assistance
    D. Soviet-bloc response to the formation of the European Economic Community

18. An important reason for the Russian Provisional Government's loss of support among Russians was that it

    A. operated a secret police force that was even more terrible than the tsar's
    B. launched an ambitious "Russification" campaign
    C. pledged to remain in World War I until it had achieved victory
    D. enacted repressive policies against free speech and assembly

19. The Duma, or elected parliament, was an idea first conceived by

    A. Peter the Great
    B. Alexander II
    C. Lenin
    D. Nicholas II

20. Each of the following has been a problem associated with the post-Soviet economy of Russia, EXCEPT

    A. modernizing transportation and industry
    B. labor productivity
    C. the development of energy resources
    D. agricultural production

21. In the war it fought from 1856-1864, Russian gained control of the northern part of

    A. Sakhalin Island
    B. the Caucasus
    C. Siberia
    D. the Crimea

22. At the time of its collapse, the Soviet Union had several factors that would help it to promote economic growth. Which of the following was NOT one of these factors?

    A. The ability to access sophisticated technology
    B. A large accumulation of capital
    C. A legal and political milieu that promoted economic productivity
    D. A highly educated and skilled work force

23. Which of the following nations was NOT created from the former Yugoslavia?

    A. Moldova
    B. Slovenia
    C. Kosovo
    D. Montenegro

24. Which of the following nations did NOT intervene militarily in the Russian Civil War?

    A. Germany
    B. Canada
    C. United States
    D. Japan

25. The Tambov Rebellion of 1919-1921 was staged against the Bolsheviks by a large number of

    A. peasants whose land had been seized
    B. Soviet sailors
    C. former tsarist officials
    D. Russian army officers

26. Which of the following was a Bolshevik whose assassination in 1934 sparked a major purge of the Communist Party leadership?

    A. Lev Kamenev
    B. Leon Trotsky
    C. Lavrentiy Beria
    D. Sergei Kirov

27. The first Balkan War was started when _____ declared war against the Ottomans in September of 1912.

    A. Bulgaria
    B. Montenegro
    C. Greece
    D. Russia

28. Which of the following was NOT an important deficiency in the Soviet Union's planned economy?

A. Overly capital-intensive methods of production.
B. Inadequate incentives to apply new technology, which contributed to slow growth.
C. Insufficient emphasis on the quality of outputs
D. A high profit incentive that steered entrepreneurs into ventures that were more specialized and less useful overall.

29. Each of the following played a significant role in bringing about the end of the Cold War, EXCEPT

    A. the overextension of the Soviet empire, combined with a stagnating economy
    B. Gorbachev's election and his plea for Western aid
    C. Ronald Reagan's acceleration of the arms race
    D. Congress's ratification of the SALT II Treaty

30. The theory of "peaceful coexistence" with capitalist states was a characteristic of the _____ regime.

    A. Khrushchev
    B. Gorbachev
    C. Brezhnev
    D. Stalin

31. From the time of Stalin's death to the collapse of the Soviet Union, economic reforms were most evident in

    A. heavy industry
    B. steel production
    C. the functions of the political system
    D. agriculture

32. Stalin's chief policy goal after World War II was to

    A. introduce some principles of the market economy
    B. extend some modest civil liberties as a show of goodwill
    C. dominate Eastern Europe
    D. eliminate ethnic tensions within the Soviet Union

33. Which of the following does NOT lie on the Baltic Sea?

    A. Latvia
    B. Poland
    C. Russia
    D. Belarus

34. The leader of the Constitutional Democratic Party was the Russian historian

    A. Pavel Miliukov
    B. Leon Trotsky
    C. Viktor Chernov
    D. Sergei Witte

35. Which of the following Soviet-bloc leaders enacted the program known as "socialism with a human face"?

A. Josip Tito of Yugoslavia
B. Nicolae Ceausescu of Romania
C. Janos Kadar of Hungary
D. Alexander Dubcek of Czechoslovakia

36. The Mingrelians wereand area n ethnographic group that lives primarily within the former Soviet republic of

    A. Kazakhstan
    B. Georgia
    C. Ukraine
    D. Azerbaijan

37. In the 1980s, the Soviet Union suffered from each of the following problems, EXCEPT

    A. insufficient oil production
    B. technological underdevelopment
    C. insufficient agricultural production
    D. industrial inefficiency

38. Among the following, the most abundant natural resource in post-Soviet Russia was

    A. natural gas
    B. fish
    C. coal
    D. oil

39. The one factor that did the most to bring about the 1861 emancipation of Russia's serfs was

    A. the tsar's growing fears of revolution
    B. Russia's defeats in the Crimean War
    C. the desire to make peasants into soldiers for the coming war
    D. the petitioning of the landed gentry in Lithuania

40. Russia's enemy in the Great Northern War of 1700-1721 was _____ , which fought with the help of _____ .

    A. Denmark-Norway, Austria
    B. Prussia, Sweden
    C. Finland, Germany
    D. Sweden, the Ottoman Empire

KEY (CORRECT ANSWERS)

1.	D	11.	A	21.	B	31.	D
2.	A	12.	A	22.	C	32.	C
3.	B	13.	D	23.	A	33.	D
4.	A	14.	C	24.	A	34.	A
5.	A	15.	B	25.	A	35.	D
6.	C	16.	A	26.	D	36.	B
7.	D	17.	D	27.	B	37.	A
8.	B	18.	C	28.	D	38.	A
9.	D	19.	B	29.	D	39.	B
10.	C	20.	C	30.	A	40.	D

EXAMINATION SECTION
TEST 1

DIRECTIONS: Each question or incomplete statement is followed by several suggested answers or completions. Select the one that BEST answers the question or completes the statement. *PRINT THE LETTER OF THE CORRECT ANSWER IN THE SPACE AT THE RIGHT.*

1. Which of the following statements about the Russian Provisional Government is FALSE? 1.____

    A. Lenin supported the Russian Provisional Government, because it had overthrown the tsar.
    B. It was Alexander Kerensky who formally declared a Russian republic.
    C. It was formed after Tsar Nicholas II abdicated peacefully.
    D. The creation of the Russian Provisional Government was praised by Woodrow Wilson

2. In 2005, the former Soviet Republic of _____ discontinued its membership in the Commonwealth of Independent States and became an associate member. 2.____

    A. Armenia
    B. Kazakhstan
    C. Georgia
    D. Turkmenistan

3. Throughout its history, the Soviet Union primarily achieved economic growth by 3.____

    A. issuing convertible currency
    B. increasing inputs
    C. joining international trade organizations
    D. encouraging investment

4. In 1939, the post of Soviet People's Commissar of Foreign Affairs was given to 4.____

    A. Nikolai Yezhov
    B. Lavrenty Beria
    C. Vyacheslav Molotov
    D. Nikita Khrushchev

5. Which of the following was NOT a change in Soviet government and politics made by Gorbachev? 5.____

    A. Allowing non-communists to run for office
    B. Making himself president
    C. Allowing greater individual freedoms in elections
    D. Legalizing an opposition party

6. The unraveling of detente between the U.S. and the Soviet Union was due to several factors, including the 6.____
    I. Soviet invasion of Afghanistan
    II. perceived loss of U.S. power and prestige during the Iran hostage crisis
    III. election of Ronald Reagan to the U.S. presidency
    IV. circulation of Charter 77 in Czechoslovakia

A. I and II
B. I, II and III
C. II and IV
D. III and IV

7. In the 1980s, the most significant factor in the movements for reform among Eastern European countries was a growing

   A. affinity for Western democratic ideas
   B. ideological rejection of communism
   C. sense of economic deprivation
   D. sense of nationalism and ethnic identity

7.____

8. The term "Weimar Russia" was coined in the mid-1990s to indicate the widespread opinion that post-Soviet Russia was

   A. populated by citizens who wanted to structure their government to resemble that of Weimar Germany
   B. a nation that would never learn democratic values
   C. poised on the brink of economic collapse due to hyperinflation
   D. a weak republic attacked from within by nationalists yearning to restore authoritarian ways

8.____

9. The "Prague Spring" of 1968 can best be described as a

   A. violent revolutionary movement
   B. limited intervention by Western powers behind the Iron Curtain
   C. form of passive resistance to Warsaw Pact troops
   D. revolt modeled after the Hungarian resistance of 1956

9.____

10. Stalin was offered the position of Communist Party Secretary because

    A. he was voted in by a small majority in party elections
    B. he had threatened to form an opposition faction within the party
    C. other prominent Bolsheviks had rejected the position
    D. he had curried favor with the leading party operatives

10.____

11. The New Economic Policy was administrated by

    A. Trotsky
    B. Bukharin
    C. Stalin
    D. Lenin

11.____

12. After 1991, the dominating factor in the lives of Caucasians became

    A. interference by European and Asian governments
    B. the loss of water resources
    C. a virtual economic collapse
    D. inter-ethnic conflict

12.____

13. The main ideological difference between the Bolsheviks and Menshe-viks was that the   13.____
    Mensheviks believed in

    A. a greater degree of popular participation in government
    B. participating in World War I until a definitive end was reached
    C. the rule of an elite proletariat
    D. private ownership of property

14. Nicholas I's doctrine of "official nationality" meant that   14.____

    A. the state would extend rights only to those citizens who publicly proclaimed them-
       selves Russian
    B. a Russian citizen was officially Russian, whatever his or her ethnic background
    C. only those Russians who came from a delimited list of certain ethnic backgrounds
       could be officially considered Russian
    D. anyone who held an appointed office in the state government had to be an ethnic
       Russian

15. The first parliamentary election after the Russian Revolution of 1905 resulted in a   15.____

    A. substantial majority for the Socialist-Revolutionary Party
    B. substantial majority for the Bolsheviks
    C. substantial majority for Alexander Kerensky
    D. resounding defeat of Marxist ideology

16. The aggressive policies masterminded by _____ encouraged the rapid industrialization   16.____
    of the Russian Empire in the 1890s.

    A. Sergei Witte
    B. V.I. Lenin
    C. Alexander III
    D. Rasputin

17. Which of the following was NOT one of Khrushchev's agricultural reforms?   17.____

    A. A massive chemical fertilizer program
    B. A retreat from collectivization
    C. The introduction of corn
    D. Rapid mechanization

18. *Pereslroika* could most accurately be described as a policy of   18.____

    A. granting political liberties to all Russians
    B. encouraging open discussions of politics and ideas
    C. removing Communist Party leaders from government
    D. restructuring the Soviet government and economy

19. The exchange rate for rubles, which in 1914 was two rubles to the dollar, had become, by   19.____
    1920, about _____ rubles to the dollar.

    A. 8
    B. 180
    C. 500
    D. 1200

20. Which of the following terms is NOT associated with the Soviet dissident movement of the 1970s and 1980s?

    A. *magniuzdat*
    B. *refusenik*
    C. *samirdat*
    D. *kukuruznik*

21. Under Peter the Great, Russia's military fought for and won a port on the

    A. Black Sea
    B. Baltic Sea
    C. Caspian Sea
    D. Arctic Ocean

22. During the 1980s, Soviet leadership had begun to conclude that Cold War competition was no longer sustainable. Which of the following was NOT a factor in this conclusion?

    A. Inferior political leadership
    B. The growing deficiency of economic performance
    C. A nuclear stalemate
    D. A widening gap in high-technology competitiveness

23. A primary reason that scholars and other observers worldwide failed to anticipate the fall of the Soviet Union was that they

    A. tended to overestimate Soviet power because of rampant anti-communism
    B. were given propaganda, instead of scientific data, to work with
    C. overemphasized politics, paying scant attention to economics
    D. did not have enough opportunities to observe the nation's inner workings

24. The Soviet economy achieved its most impressive growth from

    A. 1918-1930
    B. 1930-1960
    C. 1960-1980
    D. 1980-1992

25. A popular policy slogan of the Brezhnev regime was

    A. "Bread and Bullets"
    B. "New Thinking"
    C. "Stability of Cadres"
    D. "No Half-Measures"

26. Which of the following statements about the Russian Revolution of 1905 is TRUE?

    A. The most significant factor seemed to be a nationalist humiliation after the Russo-Japanese War.
    B. It resulted from the dissatisfactions of many different groups.
    C. After it was over, the Bolsheviks effectively controlled the government.
    D. It was almost entirely a rural, working-class movement.

27. The most obvious result of the general relaxation of authoritarianism under the rule of Brezhnev was

    A. increased economic productivity
    B. warmer relations with the United States
    C. corruption and dissent
    D. an end to the imprisonment of dissidents

28. Each of the following factors would become a principal reason for the abolition of serfdom in Russia, EXCEPT for the concern that

    A. there was an escalating danger of a serf revolt
    B. volunteer armies were superior to serf armies
    C. an indentured and immobile population would slow the process of industrialization
    D. serfdom was an immoral institution, tantamount to slavery

29. Compared to the United States's worldwide system of alliances, the Soviet Union's Warsaw Pact

    A. later required membership from its former enemy states
    B. was a strictly compulsory arrangement
    C. included nations from both the Eastern and Western hemispheres
    D. had extremely limited global power

30. As soon as Stalin had effective control of the Soviet Union, he immediately set about

    A. building up the military
    B. improving internal communications
    C. making changes to agriculture and industry
    D. implementing a police state

31. After the fall of the Soviet Union, the Russian Republic fought a bloody, unpopular and indecisive war in _____ to suppress its demands for independence.

    A. Azerbaijan
    B. Bosnia
    C. Chechnya
    D. Yugoslavia

32. The Soviet Union became a global naval power for the first time under the leadership of

    A. Stalin
    B. Malenkov
    C. Khrushchev
    D. Brezhnev

33. In 1940 the Soviet Union annexed Bessarabia, creating the Moldovan SSR out of the area that had belonged to

    A. Latvia
    B. Poland
    C. Bulgaria
    D. Romania

34. Each of the following was a result of Gorbachev's re-creation of the Congress of People's Deputies, EXCEPT   34.____

    A. the emergence of reform candidates
    B. the fall of some party leaders
    C. the end of communism
    D. free elections

35. Prior to the 1980s, one of the most significant effects of the Five-Year Plans was a   35.____

    A. surplus of manufactured goods
    B. failure to execute agricultural plans
    C. decline in military spending
    D. scarcity of consumer goods

36. Stalin's view of communism differed from that of Lenin, in that   36.____

    A. Stalin focused more on a nationalist version of communism that concentrated power
    B. Lenin was an egalitarian who wanted to include citizens from all walks of life in the communist movement
    C. Stalin questioned the necessity of the Communist Party apparatus
    D. Lenin was primarily a revolutionary who had no interest in applying communist principles to government

37. The primary significance of Lenin's New Economic Policy (NEP) was that it called for the   37.____

    A. resumption of limited private ownership
    B. equal distribution of all private property
    C. improvement and expansion of public housing
    D. collectivization of the Soviet economy

38. Russian Premier Khrushchev abruptly left the 1960 Paris Summit in May primarily because   38.____

    A. he and Eisenhower could not settle the Berlin issue
    B. he heard rumors of an attempted coup in Moscow
    C. Eisenhower refused to apologize for the U-2 incident
    D. the U.S. had launched airlifts into East Berlin

39. The expansion of the Russian Empire resembled other colonial conquests in Asia and the Americas in that it   39.____

    A. was driven primarily by religious missionary zeal
    B. imposed European institutions on indigenous systems
    C. was primarily an exercise in naval power
    D. demonstrated the advantages of modernization on remote societies

40. In its transition to a market system, Russia experienced the significant problem(s) of   40.____
    I. corruption
    II. declining output
    III. increased military spending
    IV. increasing life expectancies

A. I only
B. I and II
C. III only
D. II, III and IV

KEY (CORRECT ANSWERS)

1. A	11. B	21. B	31. C
2. D	12. D	22. A	32. D
3. B	13. A	23. C	33. D
4. C	14. B	24. B	34. C
5. A	15. A	25. C	35. D
6. B	16. A	26. B	36. A
7. D	17. B	27. C	37. A
8. D	18. D	28. D	38. C
9. C	19. D	29. D	39. B
10. C	20. D	30. C	40. B

TEST 2

DIRECTIONS: Each question or incomplete statement is followed by several suggested answers or completions. Select the one that BEST answers the question or completes the statement. *PRINT THE LETTER OF THE CORRECT ANSWER IN THE SPACE AT THE RIGHT.*

1. Immediately after World War II, the Soviets pushed for influence in each of the following countries, EXCEPT

    A. Greece
    B. Afghanistan
    C. Iran
    D. Turkey

1.____

2. Ultimately, the political fall of Alexander Kerensky was due to

    A. the rise of the Mensheviks
    B. his distribution of arm to Petrograd workers
    C. his refusal to withdraw Russia from World War I
    D. the Kornilov coup

2.____

3. When the Russian Revolution began, V.I. Lenin was about _____ years of age.

    A. 25
    B. 40
    C. 50
    D. 65

3.____

4. Each of the following was an effect of detente in the Soviet Union, EXCEPT

    A. Western criticism of the Soviet political system
    B. a greater desire among Soviet citizens for political liberty
    C. a growing resentment of police power
    D. numerous demonstrations in support of individual civil liberties

4.____

5. The last country to have been incorporated as a Soviet Socialist Republic was

    A. Estonia
    B. Kazakhstan
    C. Moldova
    D. Uzbekistan

5.____

6. Which of the following was NOT a cause of the collapse of communism in East Germany?

    A. Corrupt leadership
    B. Public demonstrations
    C. Censorship
    D. Free elections

6.____

7. Which of the following is TRUE of Lenin and his successors in the Soviet Union?

7.____

A. They began to implement the soviet system immediately after the revolution of 1906.
B. They developed a practical implementation of Marxism with no detailed example of a communist society to follow.
C. They were given a great advantage in their inheritance of a large, established, and progressive agricultural system.
D. They were supported in their efforts to establish a socialist economy by other nations that were suffering economically in the wake of World War I.

8. A major reason for the 1979 Soviet invasion of Afghanistan was   8._____

   A. the 1978 coup that overthrew the Afghan government
   B. the recent election of Jimmy Carter to the U.S. presidency
   C. a growing militancy within the Soviet Union"s Muslim republics
   D. the desire for more oil revenues to fuel industrialization

9. After Gorbachev discarded the Brezhnev Doctrine, the first country to throw out its communist regime was   9._____

   A. Czechoslovakia
   B. Poland
   C. East Germany
   D. Romania

10. After Lenin's death, Stalin's main target for removal from power was   10._____

    A. Kerensky
    B. Trotsky
    C. Bukharin
    D. Kamenev

11. The Russian Law Code of 1649   11._____

    A. merged peasants and slaves into the serf class
    B. established the hereditary nature of title of nobility
    C. exempted nobles from paying taxes
    D. allowed anyone who could afford an education to obtain one

12. Which of the following Bolshevik concepts was developed by Lenin but NOT found in the works of Marx?   12._____

    A. The violence of a workers' revolution is regrettable, but necessary.
    B. Just as feudalism yielded to capitalism, capitalism will be conquered by communism.
    C. The working class, tired of being exploited, must rise up.
    D. The communist elite will direct a "dictatorship of the proletariat."

13. The most likely reason that Russia had a more difficult time than Central European countries in making the transition to representative democracy and a free market is that unlike these countries, Russia   13._____

    A. rejected Western assistance
    B. was a religiously orthodox, rather than secular, society
    C. had based its communist rule on appeals to a powerful Russian nationalism

D. did not retain enough native talent to execute the transition

14. From the beginning of the post-World War II economy to the collapse of the Soviet Union, the role of women could be described as

    A. occupying a large number of professional positions, such as physicians and scientists, but being paid far less than their male counterparts
    B. nonexistent politically, but in time of greater significance in the economy
    C. steadily diminishing over time to occupy mostly domestic roles
    D. providing leadership on local councils, but not well-represented in national civil service positions

15. Essentially, the Warsaw Pact was terminated by the

    A. formation of NATO
    B. collapse of the Eastern European communist governments in 1989
    C. reunification of Germany in 1990
    D. collapse of the Soviet Union in 1991

16. The event that prompted the formation of the Warsaw Pact was the NATO membership of

    A. Norway
    B. the United Kingdom
    C. Germany
    D. Denmark

17. In response to the movements for independence among the Soviet republics, Gorbachev proposed a compromise confederation in 1991 called the

    A. United States of Russia
    B. Treaty of Union
    C. Federation of Soviets
    D. Commonwealth of Independent States

18. The most important area of Cold War military competition between the Soviet Union and the United States involved the production of

    A. long-range nuclear missiles
    B. stealth bombers
    C. short-range nuclear missiles
    D. nuclear-armed submarines

19. The most negative aspect of the Cold War era in the Soviet Union was the

    A. economic sanctions of Western nations
    B. increasing reluctance to engage in international cooperation
    C. fear and discouragement of the general population
    D. economic toll of maintaining the arms race

20. Alexander II's "Great Reforms" included
    I. emancipation of the serfs
    II. a more independent judicial system
    III. the creation of locally elected political assemblies
    IV. reduced military service

A. I only
B. I and II
C. II and III
D. I, II, III and IV

21. Under Brezhnev, Mikhail Gorbachev held the post of

    A. First Secretary for Agriculture
    B. Second Secretary of the Communist Party
    C. KGB head
    D. Foreign Minister

22. In 1864, a new institution of local government, the _____, was established in Russia.

    A. *soviet*
    B. *duma*
    C. *zemsivo*
    D. *kolklioze*

23. In 1917, Josef Stalin was the

    A. editor of *Pravda*
    B. Head of Propaganda
    C. chief deputy to Lenin
    D. Communist Party Secretary

24. The eminent Soviet nuclear physicist who later became a dissident and wrote "Reflections on Progress, Coexistence, and Individual Freedom" in 1968 was

    A. Mikhail Trepashkin
    B. Vladimir Bukovsky
    C. Alexander Solzhenitsyn
    D. Andrei Sakharov

25. Intellectuals who were initially attracted to the Soviet system later rejected it largely because of

    A. its failure to increase industrial output
    B. their distaste for such a highly centralized economic system
    C. its failure to improve the quality of life for working-class Russians
    D. the purges and terror of Stalin's regime

26. For Mikhail Gorbachev, one of the fatal consequences of his reforms was that they

    A. were vastly unpopular
    B. invited graft and corruption
    C. strengthened the Communist Party
    D. reduced his own power

27. Each of the following occurred as a result of the end of the Cold War, EXCEPT the

    A. return of Moldova to Romania
    B. peaceable separation of the Czech Republic and Slovakia
    C. bloody collapse of Yugoslavia

D. reunification of Germany

28. When Gerald Ford and Leonid Brezhnev met in Vladivostok in 1974, one of the major points of conflict between the U.S. and the Soviet Union was

   A. the postwar boundaries of Eastern and Central Europe
   B. each nation's stock of intercontinental ballistic missiles (ICBMs)
   C. the right of Soviet Jews and intellectuals to emigrate
   D. the extent of the Soviet Union's covert involvement in the Vietnam War

29. By the mid-19th century, the Russian Empire's interest in Central Asia was stimulated mostly by the desire to control the production of

   A. grain
   B. steel
   C. caviar
   D. cotton

30. Lenin's vision of the Bolshevik party was that it would

   A. support fighting in World War I until Germany was defeated
   B. be an elite group of professional revolutionaries who could lead the masses
   C. support the Provisional Government during a difficult transition period
   D. be a democratic group of workers

31. After World War II, Stalin's chief policy goal was

   A. the rapid growth in agricultural production
   B. to use any principles, capitalist or socialist, to expand the economy and win the Cold War
   C. Soviet domination of Eastern Europe
   D. the forced "Russianization' of the more remote Soviet republics

32. The Soviet Union made some experimental modifications to its command economy in the 1980s when it

   A. legalized trade unions
   B. eliminated central planning
   C. introduced some market economy strategies
   D. allowed some private ownership of major industries

33. The social and political reforms in Russia in the 1860s could best be described as

   A. a set of halfway measures that compounded class tensions
   B. a desperate and cynical political ploy by the monarchy
   C. revolutionary in their conception and execution
   D. an extremely effective set of pragmatic solutions to working-class problems

34. One of the most popular dissident publications, secretly disseminated in the Soviet Union during the Brezhnev era, was

   A. *Isvestia*
   B. The Gulag Archipelago
   C. *The Chronicle of Current Events*

D. *Trud*

35. Of the following, the best description of Lenin's New Economic Policy was that, in his mind, it was

    A. a temporary compromise with capitalist economic policies
    B. an affirmation that the principles of War Communism would translate easily to a peacetime economy
    C. a kind of "shock treatment" for converting the feudal economy to socialist principles
    D. a political ploy to gain favor with Marxist Bolsheviks

36. The "Winter War" of November 1939 was fought between the Soviet Union and

    A. Poland
    B. Japan
    C. Finland
    D. Norway

37. As Russia made its transition to a market economy, hyperinflation was caused by
    I. "ruble overhang," or an excess of purchasing power in house holds
    II. government deficits
    III. the lifting of price controls
    IV. land reforms

    A. I only
    B. II and III
    C. I, II and III
    D. I, II, III and IV

38. The original Marxist ideology contained the element of the

    A. oligarchy of the business class
    B. government creation of surplus value
    C. labor theory of value
    D. ownership of private property

39. A major weakness of the Soviet system until the 1980s was the

    A. military
    B. agricultural system
    C. Communist Party bureaucracy
    D. industrial and manufacturing sector

40. In the Russian revolution's early stages, Soviets were

    A. revolutionary workers' councils
    B. individual Duma representatives
    C. local governing bodies
    D. collective farms

KEY (CORRECT ANSWERS)

1. B	11. A	21. A	31. C
2. C	12. B	22. C	32. C
3. C	13. C	23. A	33. A
4. D	14. A	24. D	34. C
5. A	15. B	25. D	35. A
6. D	16. C	26. D	36. C
7. B	17. B	27. A	37. C
8. C	18. A	28. C	38. C
9. B	19. D	29. D	39. B
10. B	20. D	30. B	40. A

TEST 3

DIRECTIONS: Each question or incomplete statement is followed by several suggested answers or completions. Select the one that BEST answers the question or completes the statement. *PRINT THE LETTER OF THE CORRECT ANSWER IN THE SPACE AT THE RIGHT.*

1. The Soviet leader who achieved military parity with the United States was   1.____

   A. Konstantin Chernenko
   B. Mikhail Gorbachev
   C. Leonid Brezhnev
   D. Nikita Khrushchev

2. The Soviet Union was expelled from the League of Nations in December of 1939 because of its   2.____

   A. blockade of Berlin
   B. attack on Finland
   C. invasion of Poland
   D. signing of the Molotov-Ribbentrop Pact with Nazi Germany

3. Lenin's desire to destroy the tsarist system was motivated primarily by   3.____

   A. a lust for power
   B. his readings of Karl Marx
   C. his family's abject poverty
   D. the execution of his brother

4. Which was NOT one of the major powers to dominate the Congress of Vienna?   4.____

   A. Austria
   B. Prussia
   C. Britain
   D. Russia

5. The initial leader of the Mensheviks was   5.____

   A. Maxim Gorky
   B. Julius Martov
   C. Matvei Muranov
   D. Grigory Zinoviev

6. The "Sino-Soviet split" that peaked in 1969 could be traced to factors that included   6.____
   I. Mao's belief that he should, after Stalin's death, have been accorded the status of the senior leader of the Communist movement
   II. Mao's belief that Khrushchev was too eager to accommodate the West
   III. Soviet alarm at the Great Leap Forward, Mao's Five-Year Plan to industrialize China
   IV. The Soviet Union's failure to support China in a border dispute with India

   A. I and II
   B. II and III
   C. II, III and IV

43

D. I, II, III and IV

7. During the Soviet era, the main strategy for achieving cultural unification was to   7._____

   A. suppress religious expressions of any kind
   B. compel education about the diverse ethnicities and customs of the Soviet people in order to foster tolerance
   C. resettle ethnic Russians throughout the more remote republics
   D. borrow from more uniformly European customs and traditions

8. Boris Yeltsin became the commanding figure in post-Soviet politics when he   8._____

   A. cracked down harshly on dissident voices against his government
   B. led a "silent coup" the effectively undercut Gorbachev's political support
   C. defeated Gorbachev soundly in a series of public debates
   D. publicly denounced an attempted coup staged by old-line communists against Gorbachev

9. Which of the following nations remained independent of direct Soviet control after 1948?   9._____

   A. Albania
   B. Hungary
   C. Czechoslovakia
   D. Poland

10. Stalin's reforms included   10._____
    I. Five-Year Plans that set economic production targets
    II. the revival of militarism and nationalism
    III. forced increases in the production of consumer goods
    IV. the confiscation and nationalization of *kulak* properties

    A. I and II
    B. I, II and IV
    C. III and IV
    D. I, II, III and IV

11. Probably the most important cause of low agricultural productivity in the Soviet Union was the   11._____

    A. overuse of chemical fertilizers and pesticides
    B. failure to provide incentives for agriculture
    C. shortage of arable land
    D. outdated technology used in farming

12. Which of the following was the term used to describe the regional councils that Khrushchev established in an effort to coordinate the operations and management of the Soviet Union's different economic regions?   12._____

    A. *politruks*
    B. *sovnarkhozes*
    C. *kukuruzniks*
    D. *kolkhozes*

13. Russian peasants reacted to the fell of the Russian government in 1917 by   13.____

    A. seizing land
    B. rioting and looting village shops
    C. obeying the requests of the Provisional government to wait for land-redistribution legislation
    D. enlisting in the military in unprecedented numbers

14. To maintain power, Stalin made use of each of the following, EXCEPT   14.____

    A. the army
    B. the secret police
    C. foreign aid
    D. the Communist Party

15. The most significant factor that led to the overthrow of Nicholas II was   15.____

    A. a powerfully united revolutionary movement
    B. how own rapid allowance of democratic reforms
    C. the strength of Russian labor unions
    D. a series of defeats in World War I

16. Marxism's criticism of capitalism was deeply rooted in capitalism's   16.____

    A. practice of levying lower relative tax rates on the wealthy
    B. sharing of surplus value with the government
    C. reduction of worker productivity by failing to invest profits in new capital
    D. failure to pay wages that equaled the value of production

17. The terms of the SALT II Treaty were   17.____
    I. never ratified by the Soviet Union
    II. never ratified by the United States because of the Soviet invasion of Afghanistan
    III. honored by both sides
    IV. ignored by both sides

    A. I and IV
    B. II and III
    C. I, II and IV
    D. IV only

18. During World War II, the Soviet Union seized control of the Far Eastern province of   18.____
    _____, which was incorporated into the Russian Soviet Federated Socialist Republic (SFSR).

    A. Mongolia
    B. Tanna-Tuva
    C. Sakha
    D. Tatarstan

19. The rapid growth and importance of the dissident movement throughout the Soviet Union   19.____
    and satellite countries in the 1980s is best explained by

A. the spread of new communications technology
   B. the relative weakness of Soviet leadership after 1975
   C. a liberalized regime under Brezhnev
   D. the growth of the black market in consumer goods

20. The Soviet Union achieved superpower status in the period 20.____

   A. 1917-1928
   B. 1928-1939
   C. 1945-1985
   D. 1985-1992

21. Soviet economic policies traditionally emphasized the production of 21.____

   A. agricultural produce
   B. durable consumer goods
   C. heavy industrial goods
   D. building materials

22. The most significant political impact of Russia's "Time of Troubles' the chaos, unrest, and 22.____
    foreign invasions that preceded the first Romanov tsar in 1613was that

   A. Russia became a decentralized country that was often governed by foreign puppet rulers
   B. a powerful grassroots movement arose that would eventually lead to the freedom of serfs
   C. the labor class became perennially disgruntled
   D. the Russian people were willing to accept autocratic rule

23. Which of the following became the head of the KGB in 1967? 23.____

   A. Vladimir Zhirinovsky
   B. Yuri Andropov
   C. Leonid Brezhnev
   D. Mikhail Gorbachev

24. Lenin's government generally 24.____

   A. ignored any opposition to its economic policies
   B. micromanaged agriculture but left industry to the private sector
   C. clung stubbornly to War Communism until long after the Civil War had ended
   D. allowed most decisions about agricultural production to be made locally

25. Both the New Economic Policy (NEP) of Vladimir Lenin and Mikhail's policy of *pere-* 25.____
    stroika sought to

   A. increase production through individual enterprise
   B. increasingly centralize economic planning
   C. reduce the influence of middle-class farmers
   D. spend lavishly on the military

26. Between 1928 and 1940, the production of the industrial sector of the Soviet economy 26.____

A. was reduced by half
B. remained about the same
C. doubled
D. quadrupled

27. Between 1924 and 1929, Stalin managed to force leading Bolsheviks out of power by   27.____

    A. arranging their "disappearances"
    B. assigning them to meaningless civil posts in far-flung republics
    C. playing opposing factions against each other until leaders were isolated
    D. arranging for the publication of libelous stories in the newspapers that ruined their reputations

28. The Khrushchev regime was characterized by   28.____
    I. modest expectations for Soviet progress
    II. a greater willingness to allow Eastern European countries to chart their own political course
    III. a staggering increase in agricultural production
    IV. an openness about the horror of Stalin

    A. I and II
    B. II, III and IV
    C. IV only
    D. I, II, III and IV

29. Each of the following was an example of the Soviet Union attempting to expand its "sphere of influence" during the 1960s, EXCEPT the   29.____

    A. Berlin Wall
    B. CubanMissile Crisis
    C. Six Day War of 1967
    D. principle of "peaceful coexistence"

30. Which of the following was a result of the Russian Revolution of 1905?   30.____

    A. An end to labor unrest
    B. The establishment of the elective assembly known as the Duma.
    C. The overthrow of the tsar
    D. a Provisional Government

31. The principal heavy-manufacturing region of the Soviet Union was in   31.____

    A. Georgia
    B. Russia
    C. Kazakhstan
    D. Ukraine

32. The dissident who was deported in 1974 for his Western publication of *The Gulag Archipelago* was   32.____

    A. Andrei Sakharov
    B. Natan Sharansky
    C. Alexander Solzhenitsyn
    D. Sergei Kovalev

33. The former Warsaw Pact nation that enjoyed the smoothest transition to democracy and a free-market economy in the post-Soviet era is

   A. Albania
   B. the Czech Republic
   C. Bulgaria
   D. Romania

33.____

34. Russia decided to support the government of the Republic of Georgia in 1994 because

   A. Georgia agreed to join the Commonwealth of Independent States
   B. Georgia withdrew its support from the Muslim Abkhazian movement
   C. there was a new Russian president
   D. Georgia abandoned its plan to re-establish a Soviet-style communist government

34.____

35. The Soviet republics that generally led the others in pressing for independence from Moscow in the late 1980s were

   A. the Baltics
   B. large Central Asian republics
   C. in the Transcaucasus
   D. on the border with Central Europe

35.____

36. In practice, the Brezhnev Doctrine meant that

   A. Western interferences in the governments or economies of Soviet satellite nations were interpreted as acts of war
   B. Moscow tacitly granted permission to its allies to decide their own futures
   C. the Soviet Union would never agree to a reduction in the buildup of its military or its arsenal
   D. the Red Army would put a stop to any Eastern European's efforts to achieve change or reform

36.____

37. Woodrow Wilson's Fourteen Points responded to Russia's concerns in each of the following ways, EXCEPT by

   A. offering terms for peace while removing the Kaiser
   B. calling for the removal of all foreign troops from Russia
   C. leaving open the possibility that the imperial agendas of Japan and Britain might be satisfied
   D. demanding open covenants

37.____

38. The main reason so many Asian and African nations followed a policy of nonalignment in the Cold War era was because they

   A. were working to establish their own democratic institutions
   B. wanted to receive aid from both the United States and the Soviet Union
   C. shared geopolitical goals with both the United States and the Soviet Union
   D. wanted foreign powers to stay out of their internal affairs

38.____

39. The most easily apparent result of Gorbachev's *glasnost* policy was

   A. the liberation of satellite nations
   B. a new round of anti-ballistic missile treaties with the United States

39.____

C. an increase in political dissent
D. the "ruble overhang"

40. Effects of Stalin's agricultural policy between 1932 and 1934 included
    I. a 30 percent increase in production
    II. the increased wealth of the corrupt kulak class
    III. a 15 percent decline in production
    IV. the deaths of 5 million citizens by starvation

    A. I only
    B. II only
    C. II and III
    D. III and IV

40.____

KEY (CORRECT ANSWERS)

1.	C	11.	B	21.	C	31.	D
2.	B	12.	B	22.	D	32.	C
3.	D	13.	A	23.	B	33.	B
4.	A	14.	C	24.	D	34.	A
5.	B	15.	D	25.	A	35.	A
6.	D	16.	D	26.	D	36.	D
7.	C	17.	B	27.	C	37.	C
8.	D	18.	B	28.	C	38.	B
9.	A	19.	A	29.	A	39.	C
10.	B	20.	C	30.	B	40.	D

TEST 4

DIRECTIONS: Each question or incomplete statement is followed by several suggested answers or completions. Select the one that BEST answers the question or completes the statement. *PRINT THE LETTER OF THE CORRECT ANSWER IN THE SPACE AT THE RIGHT.*

1. Each of the following is a significant reason why the Whites lost the Russian Civil War, EXCEPT that they 1.____

    A. had little popular support among
    B. lacked strong leadership
    C. were too exclusive and elitist in their ideology
    D. were divided ideologically

2. When the Bolsheviks failed to win a majority in the elections of November 12, 1917, Lenin ordered the Red Army to 2.____

    A. arrest key leaders of the Socialist Revolutionaries
    B. seize control of the Duma
    C. disperse the Constituent Assembly
    D. seize the ballot boxes

3. The first former Warsaw Pact member to join NATO was 3.____

    A. Hungary
    B. Poland
    C. the Czech Republic
    D. East Germany as a part of reunified Germany

4. In the mid-19th century, Tsar Alexander II 4.____

    A. established a system of free public education
    B. freed the serfs and introduced some government reforms
    C. took land away from the nobles
    D. established safety and other labor reforms in industrial factories

5. During the 1920s, under Stalin's orders, the Soviet Bloc nations' general approach to socialist reformers was to 5.____

    A. form political alliances with Socialists in order to win leadership positions in elections
    B. avoid alliances with them, as they represented the bourgeoisie
    C. accept help in achieving reforms wherever they could find it
    D. marginalize or even eliminate them if they became troublesome

6. Of the territories occupied by the Soviets in 1940, which had NOT bordered the Soviet Union before the 1939 annexation of eastern Poland? 6.____

    A. Lithuania
    B. Karelia
    C. Bessarabia
    D. Estonia

7. Former Soviet republics that joined the Commonwealth of Independent States (CIS) include
   I. Belarus
   II. Latvia
   III. Ukraine
   IV. Kazakhstan

   A. I only
   B. I and II
   C. I, II and III
   D. I, II, III and IV

8. Because it occurred without bloodshed, the fall of communism in _____ was called the "Velvet Revolution."

   A. Poland
   B. Romania
   C. Czechoslovakia
   D. Yugoslavia

9. Khrushchev's most significant domestic failure was committed in the field of

   A. agriculture
   B. industrial output
   C. roads and transport
   D. scientific research

10. In 1991, the _____ became the first to secede from Yugoslavia because the communist leadership refused to establish economic and political liberalization.

    A. Serbs
    B. Croatians
    C. Bosnians
    D. Slovenians

11. The most significant aspect of Lenin's 1922 "political testament" was its

    A. renunciation of Bolshevism
    B. praise of Trotsky
    C. demand for further land reforms
    D. pointed criticism of Stalin

12. The Soviet attempt to industrialize Siberia was hampered by the
    I. lack of natural resources
    II. harshness of the climate and landscape
    III. insufficiency of the regional labor supply
    IV. expense of establishing a transport system

    A. I and II
    B. I, II and III
    C. II, III and IV
    D. I, II, III and IV

13. Generally, Catherine the Great's attempts to implement her enlightened ideals throughout the Russian Empire resulted in

    A. increased subjugation of the peasantry
    B. a period of relative peace and stability
    C. a new constitution
    D. dramatic increases in agricultural production

14. In 1988, Gorbachev publicly replaced the Brezhnev Doctrine with what he called the _____ Doctrine.

    A. Solidarity
    B. Warsaw
    C. Velvet Curtain
    D. Sinatra

15. Stalin's agriculture policy resulted in

    A. a state-planned system that did not produce much surplus
    B. an unplanned market economy among the kulaks
    C. a drain of labor from his industrialization program
    D. land redistribution to private owners

16. The Soviet Union's invasion of Hungary in 1956, as well as the building of the Berlin Wall, were events which illustrated

    A. the military weakness of NATO
    B. failures of the Truman Doctrine
    C. the aftereffects of the Marshall Plan
    D. proof of the "domino theory"

17. In 1988, Soviet military forces had to step in to calm the ethnic violence between the republics of

    A. Lithuania and Latvia
    B. Georgia and Ukraine
    C. Azerbaijan and Armenia
    D. Kazakhstan and Turkmenistan

18. In terms of the dissident movement, the publication of *The Gulag Archipelago* in 1973 would best be described as a

    A. pseudonym
    B. *samizdat*
    C. khrushchovka
    D. *tamizdat*

19. Which of the following is LEAST likely to be considered a factor that contributed to the start of the Cold War?

    A. U.S. weakness at Yalta
    B. Rapid U.S. post-war military demobilization
    C. Soviet quest for spheres of influence
    D. Soviet pressures on the Yugoslavian regime

20. The first Eastern European country to gain substantial independence from the Soviet Union after World War II was

   A. Poland
   B. Albania
   C. Yugoslavia
   D. Romania

20.____

21. The major factor that led to the end of the Cold War was the

   A. low standard of living and quality of life in the Soviet Union compared to the West
   B. disorder caused by the democratization of the political system
   C. relationship of trust between Ronald Reagan and Mikhail Gorbachev
   D. irreversible decline in Soviet military power

21.____

22. In March of 1940, the Soviet Union established the _____ Republic near the border of Finland in order to assert Soviet claims to Finnish land.

   A. Finno-Karelian Soviet Socialist
   B. Finnish Democratic
   C. Karelian Socialist
   D. Karelian Autonomous Soviet Socialist

22.____

23. Reasons for the failure of Khaishchev's Virgin Lands Campaign included
   I. monocultural reliance on wheat
   II. the selection of nutrient-poor tracts of soil
   III. a lack of silos for storing the grain produced
   IV. the importation of non-native Ukrainians into the Kazakh SSR to farm

   A. I only
   B. I and III
   C. II and III
   D. I, II, III and IV

23.____

24. The Mensheviks believed that

   A. the working class should seize power and hasten the revolution
   B. socialism would be brought to Russia only through the work of the peasants
   C. socialism should be a gradual process, chosen as the best among many options
   D. because of the way Marx had predicted history, capitalism would be a necessary stage in the progression of the new Russian state

24.____

25. Which of the following were LEAST likely to oppose Gorbachev's reforms?

   A. State employees
   B. Communist Party officials
   C. Police informers
   D. Dissidents

25.____

26. In the last years of the Soviet economy, just prior to its collapse, real outputs

   A. declined dramatically
   B. declined slightly
   C. increased dramatically

26.____

D. remained stable

27. The *apparatchiks* and *nomenklatura* responded to *perestroika* by

    A. shifting their support to Yeltsin
    B. sabotaging it through hoarding
    C. launching a vigorous public campaign against it
    D. converting rubles to Euros

28. Nicholas II's decision in 1905 to _____ had the effect of further weakening the Russian monarchy.

    A. issue a number of economic reforms
    B. take personal command of the army
    C. build a new palace in Petersburg
    D. mobilize Russian troops

29. The post-Soviet economy faced each of the following significant challenges, EXCEPT

    A. increasing labor productivity
    B. increasing agricultural production
    C. modernizing industry and transport
    D. developing more energy resources

30. The post-Cold War Soviet reform program included each of the following, EXCEPT

    A. *glasnost*
    B. *raion*
    C. *uskeronie*
    D. *perestroika*

31. The first Russian ruler to attempt to Westernize and modernize Russia was

    A. TsarFyodor II
    B. Peter the Great
    C. Nicholas I
    D. Catherine the Great

32. Each of the following was a factor that forced Nicholas II to adopt reforms, EXCEPT

    A. a general strike that ground the economy to a halt
    B. Bloody Sunday in 1905
    C. the October Manifesto
    D. the loss of the Russo-Japanese War

33. The Soviet policy that caused the most severe escalation in Cold War tensions was the

    A. formation of "people's republics" in Eastern Europe
    B. dissemination of propaganda that blamed "imperialist" powers for international crises
    C. practice of espionage in the West that led to the buildup of its on nuclear arsenal
    D. refusal to repay its obligations under the Lend-Lease Act

34. After the collapse of the Soviet Union, the former republic with the LEAST potential for industrialization was

    A. Ukraine
    B. Belarus
    C. Russia
    D. Kazakhstan

35. In 1990, the Soviet Union refused to recognize a reunited Germany as part of the

    A. International Nuclear Non-proliferation Treaty (NPT)
    B. NATO
    C. Warsaw Pact
    D. European Community

36. The post-Stalin foreign policy announced by Khrushchev rested on the principle of

    A. peaceful coexistence
    B. brinkmanship
    C. detente
    D. mutually assured destruction

37. The fundamental causes for the widespread stagnation of the Soviet economy under Brezhnev included the
    I. inability of the state-governed industrial economy to modernize or innovate
    II. inability of the Soviet agricultural system to feed urban areas
    III. "informal economy" that provided a market for consumer goods and services
    IV. official corruption

    A. I and II
    B. III only
    C. II and III
    D. I, III and IV

38. Leon Trotsky was the first head of the

    A. Red Army
    B. Cheka, or secret police
    C. Politburo
    D. Gospian

39. A major element of Gorbachev's policy of *perestroika* was

    A. the redistribution of wealth
    B. greater reliance on regional and local decision-making
    C. collective farming
    D. wholesale privatization of major industries

40. Throughout its history, the most pervasive characteristic of the Soviet Union was its

    A. centralized planning
    B. consumer sovereignty
    C. market system
    D. ideological purity

KEY (CORRECT ANSWERS)

1. C	11. D	21. A	31. B
2. C	12. C	22. A	32. C
3. D	13. A	23. B	33. A
4. B	14. D	24. D	34. D
5. B	15. A	25. D	35. D
6. A	16. B	26. A	36. A
7. D	17. C	27. B	37. A
8. C	18. D	28. B	38. A
9. A	19. D	29. D	39. B
10. D	20. C	30. B	40. A

EXAMINATION SECTION
TEST 1

DIRECTIONS: Each question or incomplete statement is followed by several suggested answers or completions. Select the one that BEST answers the question or completes the statement. *PRINT THE LETTER OF THE CORRECT ANSWER IN THE SPACE AT THE RIGHT.*

1. Stalin's IMMEDIATE response to the German invasion of the Soviet Union in 1941 was to   1.____

    A. coordinate a secret counteroffensive through the Caucasus
    B. go into seclusion for several days
    C. appeal to the Allies for assistance
    D. publicly rally the population around the socialist cause

2. The food crisis that existed when the Bolsheviks seized power in 1917 persisted for several years afterward, mostly because   2.____

    A. a widespread drought was killing off many Russian crops
    B. surplus stores of grain were hoarded by thuggish overlords in rural areas
    C. most Russian grain was being exported to support the expansion of Bolshevik power
    D. peasants were given no incentive to produce under War Communism's requisition policies

3. In 1986, the Soviet Union and Japan had no working peace agreement because of   3.____

    A. lingering tensions from the Soviet destruction of a commercial airliner just north of Japan
    B. the Soviet occupation of four northern Japanese islands since World War II
    C. the Japanese refusal to cede all of Sakhalin Island
    D. the lack of a formal treaty after the Russo-Japanese War

4. In 1926, a *United Opposition* was formed within the Communist Party. Against whom was this opposition united?   4.____

    A. Stalin
    B. Gorky
    C. Trotsky
    D. Zinoviev and Kamenev

5. Which of the following were principles adopted at the 1966 23rd Party Congress, led by Brezhnev and Kosygin?   5.____
    I. An economic program that emphasized defense production and heavy industry
    II. A relaxation of artistic and ideological controls
    III. An end to the discussion of human rights abuses that occurred under Stalin
    The CORRECT answer is:

    A. I, III
    B. II *only*
    C. II, III
    D. I, II, III

6. A large subdivision of a Soviet republic, comparable to a province, was known as a(n)   6.____

    A. Raion   B. Balkan   C. Soyuz   D. Oblast

57

7. In late nineteenth-century Russia, the commune system that was established after the emancipation of the peasantry proved to be relatively unproductive. The main reason for this was because the

   A. majority of peasants did not have hereditary tenure and therefore had no interest in developing the land
   B. nobles still controlled the flow of capital resources into the communes
   C. population was increasing at a rate that could not be supported by family farming
   D. political alliances among commune leaders were mostly corrupt and siphoned off much of the profits

8. Which of the following was the first country to accept Soviet gold in the period following the 1917 revolution?

   A. Japan   B. Sweden   C. Italy   D. Norway

9. For what reason was Soviet secret police chief Lavrenti Beria tried and executed in 1953?

   A. Other Soviet leaders felt threatened by his power.
   B. He was a spy working for the British.
   C. He protested Krushchev's policy of de-Stalinization.
   D. He was one of the Jews implicated in the *Doctors' Plot*.

10. The New Economic Policy (NEP) declared by Lenin in 1921 was, first and foremost, a(n) _____ policy.

    A. investment   B. agrarian
    C. industrial   D. social engineering

11. The Rapallo Treaty of 1922 marked the establishment of diplomatic relations between the Soviet Republic and

    A. Orgburo   B. Central Committee
    C. Politburo   D. Supreme Soviet

12. Throughout the Soviet era, the most powerful body within the Communist Party of the Soviet Union (CPSU) was the

    A. Orgburo   B. Central Committee
    C. Politburo   D. Supreme Soviet

13. The reign of Alexander III (1881-1894) can be most accurately characterized as

    A. a period of cautious reform whose slow pace further angered revolutionaries
    B. economic stagnation caused by the retrenchment of industrial capabilities
    C. a harsh police state designed to re-establish autocracy
    D. a country preoccupied with foreign wars to the neglect of domestic issues

14. The short-term effect of the 1967 Six-Day War on Soviet foreign relations was

    A. Arab skepticism of Soviet resolve
    B. improved diplomatic relations with Israel
    C. increased Soviet involvement in building the Arab militaries
    D. a strengthening of cooperation with the West

15. Which of the following was NOT an idea that was characteristic of the *changing landmarks* movement of the 1920s? The

    A. Bolsheviks were the embodiment of the Russian spirit and would achieve the ultimate stability of the nation
    B. revolution had been halted by the Soviet government, which was proceeding to carry out programs
    C. evolution from radicalism to empire would proceed as it had after the French revolution
    D. Russian revolution was fundamentally a nationalist revolution with Slavic roots

16. The USSR's quota-driven command economy was in operation to some degree from the year _____ to the fall of the Soviet Union.

    A. 1918   B. 1921   C. 1929   D. 1934

17. Among the factors that permitted the Bolsheviks' relatively bloodless takeover of the Winter Palace in the fall of 1917, the most significant was

    A. their appeal to the peasantry
    B. the lack of resistance from the military
    C. their ability to appease the landed aristocracy
    D. the brilliance of Lenin and Trotsky

18. The 1961 Vienna meetings between Kennedy and Krushchev were focused primarily on the issue of

    A. the Cuban missile crisis
    B. nuclear arms reduction in general
    C. Communist China's world role
    D. Germany and Berlin

19. The primary focus of Stalin's first Five-Year Plan was

    A. an increase in labor productivity
    B. the qualitative improvement of goods
    C. the integration of peasants into urban population structures
    D. an increase in output totals

20. Each of the following was an issue that received significant attention at the 1967 Glassboro Summit between Lyndon Johnson and Premier Kosygin EXCEPT

    A. the Middle East
    B. nuclear nonproliferation
    C. Germany and Berlin
    D. Vietnam

21. What was the term used for senior members of the Communist Party of the Soviet Union who held the most important positions in the government and who received substantial material benefits in return for their loyalty?

    A. Mensheviks
    B. Apparatchiks
    C. Procurators
    D. The Communist Bourgeoisie

22. Russia's great 19th-century southern trade had its foundation in

    A. St. Petersburg
    B. the rail lines branching out of Irkutsk

C. the Black Sea port of Odessa
D. Astrakhan, at the delta of the Volga River

23. Under the 12th Five-Year Plan, launched in 1985, economic growth was to be accomplished chiefly by

   A. greater foreign investment
   B. greater productivity and higher technology
   C. revenues from steel and arms exports
   D. increased employment in the defense sector

24. The _____ represented the first – and last – collaboration between the Soviet government and members of the intelligentsia?

   A. All-Russia Famine Relief Committee
   B. Council of People's Commissars
   C. Volunteer Army
   D. Central Executive Committee

25. At the Potsdam conference of 1945, United States President Truman was not as conciliatory toward Stalin as his predecessor, Roosevelt, had been. The main reason for this was that

   A. Truman was generally a more forceful personality than Roosevelt
   B. the new British Prime Minister, Clement Attlee, was urging Truman to exclude the Soviets from the war effort against Japan
   C. Truman knew the atomic bomb had been developed
   D. Stalin's designs on Eastern Europe had been made clearer

26. In 1931, the Central Committee passed a resolution calling for the return of Soviet schools to the old methods, courses, lessons, and themes that had been condemned by the revolution. The reason for this was because

   A. fewer and fewer students were attending classes
   B. experiments in education had been branded as *leftist deviations*
   C. it was believed that the schools were becoming too regimented and stifling
   D. Stalin had succeeded in rewriting the history that would be taught in schools

27. Who was the first top Soviet leader to visit the United States?

   A. Stalin   B. Krushchev   C. Brezhnev   D. Gorbachev

28. Which of the following contributed to the overall failure of the revolutionary movement of 1905?

   I. Inability to mobilize support in rural areas
   II. The splitting of the opposition over the issue of the Duma
   III. The return of loyalist armed forces from the Far East
   IV. The disabling of communications networks effected by general strikes

   The CORRECT answer is:

   A. I, II   B. II, III
   C. I, III, IV   D. I, II, III, IV

29. The main reason for the slow pace of Gorbachev's early reforms was that he
    A. encountered strong resistance from a suspicious populace
    B. needed time to consolidate his power in the party
    C. did not want to give the impression that the country was weak and in need of reform
    D. was not yet sure that wholesale reforms would solve the country's problems

30. The original Union of Soviet Socialist Republics, established in 1922, included the _____ republic.
    A. Estonian   B. Ukrainian   C. Uzbek   D. Georgian

31. Who was elected president of the Russian republic in 1990 and promised to create a market economy in 500 days?
    A. Grigory Yavlinsky   B. Aleksandr Rutskoy
    C. Boris Yeltsin   D. Nikolai Ryzhkov

32. Which of the following countries did NOT declare war on the Ottoman Empire in 1912?
    A. Greece   B. Bulgaria   C. Romania   D. Serbia

33. Approximately what percentage of the total population of the Soviet Union was killed during World War II?
    A. 3   B. 7   C. 12   D. 20

34. Russian history proper can be said to begin
    A. along the eastern shores of the Gulf of Finland, including the area of present-day St. Petersburg
    B. in the city of Moscow and along the River Volga from its mouth to the Caspian Sea
    C. in the alluvial plains just west of the Ural mountains
    D. along the northern shore of the Black Sea and in the steppe beyond

35. Who was named president of the Soviet Union at a July 2, 1985 session of the Supreme Soviet?
    A. Grigory Romanov   B. Mikhail Gorbachev
    C. Yegor Ligachev   D. Andrei Gromyko

36. The main difference between the 1924 constitution and the one drafted by Stalin in 1936 was that Stalin's constitution
    A. granted a greater degree of freedom to Russians
    B. explicitly outlawed all parties but the Communists
    C. explicitly denied clergymen the right to vote
    D. disavowed the use of terror

37. Though originally an *umbrella* word applied to Gorbachev's entire reform program came to be applied primarily in reference to
    A. government accountability   B. economic reform
    C. defense restructuring   D. social reform

38. From the turn of the century, which of the following structures evolved most slowly in Russia?

    A. Economic
    C. Governmental
    B. Social
    D. Cultural

39. Krushchev's 1954 *Virgin Lands* program can best be described as a(n)

    A. risky fringe experiment that had little impact on actual grain production numbers
    B. temporary relief from an agrarian crisis that offered no solution to the problem of productivity
    C. permanent lift to the Soviet agricultural economy that both boosted production and improved the employment rate
    D. unqualified failure that temporarily wiped out the national grain crop and necessitated several years of imports

40. Which of the following did NOT become a member of the Commonwealth of Independent States (CIS)?

    A. Moldova   B. Armenia   C. Estonia   D. Kirghizstan

KEY (CORRECT ANSWERS)

1. B	11. A	21. B	31. C
2. D	12. C	22. C	32. C
3. B	13. C	23. B	33. C
4. A	14. A	24. A	34. D
5. A	15. A	25. C	35. D
6. D	16. C	26. B	36. B
7. A	17. B	27. B	37. B
8. B	18. D	28. B	38. C
9. A	19. D	29. B	39. B
10. B	20. C	30. B	40. C

TEST 2

DIRECTIONS: Each question or incomplete statement is followed by several suggested answers or completions. Select the one that BEST answers the question or completes the statement. *PRINT THE LETTER OF THE CORRECT ANSWER IN THE SPACE AT THE RIGHT.*

1. The Chinese response to Krushchev's conduct of the 1956 20th Party Congress could best be described as one of

   A. fear   B. confusion   C. approbation   D. disgust

2. Which of the following groups was a Turkic minority within the Soviet Union?

   A. Ingush   B. Kalmyks   C. Azeris   D. Karachai

3. The Socialist Revolutionary Party, or SRP, was founded in 1902 by

   A. Russian nationalists who wanted revolution of the peasantry but supported policies of Russification
   B. nihilists who wanted an end to all forms of government in Russia
   C. non-Marxist dissidents committed to peasant revolution
   D. the Mensheviks committed to the gradual emancipation of the proletariat

4. The elections in March of 1989 to the new legislature of the USSR were surprising to Gorbachev and other government leaders because

   A. the delegates elected were overwhelmingly conservative and anti-reform
   B. there was strong evidence of many elections having been rigged in favor of Communist Party candidates
   C. there was an unexpectedly low voter turnout
   D. the Communist Party had not performed as well as expected

5. Approximately what percentage of the Russian population starved in the 1921 famine?

   A. 3   B. 12   C. 20   D. 33

6. For what reason was the Soviets' 1956 invasion of Hungary not protested strongly by the international community?

   A. It was a secret invasion that lasted only several hours.
   B. Hungary was already thought to be lost to Communism.
   C. It was a relatively bloodless suppression.
   D. Most governments were already preoccupied with the invasion of the Suez Canal.

7. The March Revolution of 1917 began spontaneously in

   A. Kiev   B. Moscow
   C. the peasant countryside   D. Petrograd

8. In his 1941 address to the Soviet people after the German invasion, Stalin justified his previous nonaggression pact with Hitler on the grounds that

   A. it ensured a strong Soviet presence in Eastern Europe after the war was over
   B. it had bought the country time to build its defenses
   C. he had believed Germany to be the lesser of two evils in the conflict
   D. he had been deceived by the fascist leader

9. The decisive moment in the August 1991 coup against Gorbachev, when it became clear that the coup would fail, came when

    A. Boris Yeltsin publicly urged the public to resist the plotters' grab for power
    B. Gorbachev resigned from his position as general secretary of the Communist party
    C. the Soviet armed forces stopped their movement toward parliament
    D. Gorbachev resurfaced from captivity

10. Despite his own efforts, Sergei Witte, Prime Minister under Nicholas II, was unable to attract liberals or moderates into his cabinet. The main reason for this was that

    A. liberals and moderates refused to support the way in which the tsar was attempting to crush the revolutionary movement
    B. both liberals and moderates were holding out for positions in the newly-created Duma, or parliament
    C. the cabinet was perceived as being a powerless institution
    D. both liberals and moderates were still opposed to the parliamentary form of government

11. In what decade did the Soviet Union achieve nuclear parity with the United States?

    A. 1940s   B. 1950s   C. 1960s   D. 1970s

12. Which of the following were members of the White forces during the civil war that began in 1918?

    I. Monarchists
    II. Liberals
    III. Conservatives
    IV. Mensheviks

    The CORRECT answer is:

    A. I, III
    B. II, IV
    C. I, III, IV
    D. I, II, III, IV

13. What was the term used to identify the right-wing group of parliamentary deputies, headed by Lt. Colonel Viktor Alksnis, that exerted influence over Gorbachev in the early 1990s?

    A. Black Berets
    B. Cossacks
    C. Soyuz
    D. Alpha Team

14. The post-revolutionary civil war in Russia began in 1918 when White forces under General Alexander Kolchak gathered in

    A. the Transcaucasus
    B. the Crimea
    C. Siberia
    D. Petrograd

15. In the period that passed between the failed coup of August 1991 and the formation of the Commonwealth of Independent States (CIS), how many of the former Soviet republics declared their independence?

    A. 5   B. 9   C. 12   D. 15

16. Which of the following was a result of the 1921 Treaty of Riga? 16.____

    A. Poland was granted control of border regions in the Ukraine and Belorussia.
    B. Japan was granted control of southern Sakhalin Island.
    C. The Baltic states remained independent.
    D. The Transcaucasus was divided into three republics.

17. Stalin's third Five-Year plan focused primarily on 17.____

    A. the stabilization of consumer prices
    B. developing the defense industries
    C. universal employment
    D. agricultural production

18. Which of the following was NOT considered to be one of the *Slavic* republics of the USSR? 18.____

    A. Russia   B. Georgia   C. Ukraine   D. Belorussia

19. Which of the following was the first Soviet republic to declare its independence from the USSR? 19.____

    A. Chechnya   B. Lithuania   C. Georgia   D. Ukraine

20. During the personnel changes made during the first months of Gorbachev's leadership, most of the officials he targeted for retirement were 20.____

    A. low-level bureaucrats
    B. rising young challengers for power in the party structure
    C. advocates of radical reform
    D. holdovers from the Brezhnev era

21. Immediately upon entering World War I in 1914, Russia's initial goals were to 21.____
    I. fulfill its defense obligation to France
    II. acquire the Turkish Straits
    III. block German and Austrian ambitions in the Balkans
    IV. acquire Constantinople
    The CORRECT answer is:

    A. I, III   B. II, III   C. II, IV   D. III, IV

22. The 1991 coup against the Gorbachev government failed because of a number of blunders on the part of the plotters. Their most significant mistake was probably 22.____

    A. taking inadequate steps to control the media
    B. overestimating the loyalty of military officers
    C. failing to arrest or silence Boris Yeltsin
    D. delaying the deployment of military support for the coup

23. Which of the following was NOT a member of the *triumvirate* elected by the Thirteenth Party Congress to assume the leadership of Lenin? 23.____

    A. Kamenev   B. Zinoviev   C. Trotsky   D. Stalin

24. Krushchev rose to power within the Communist Party after Stalin's death by advocating

    A. a reconcentration on heavy industry and the military
    B. improvements in education and medical care
    C. a shifting focus toward the production of consumer goods
    D. agricultural reforms

25. During the era of the New Economic Policy, the most important economic force in Russia were the

    A. industrialists   B. railroads   C. Nepmen   D. peasants

26. At the time of Gorbachev's reforms, most reformers in the government advocated

    A. the independence of several republics
    B. price supports for consumer goods
    C. greater republican autonomy
    D. the stable presence of the Communist party

27. Which of the following were the earliest rulers of southern Russia?

    A. Huns   B. Mongols   C. Scythians   D. Goths

28. The *secret additional protocol of* the 1939 nonaggression pact between Germany and the Soviet Union concerned an agreement to

    A. divide up Eastern Europe at the end of the war
    B. lend Russian naval support in the German offensive against Britain
    C. overlook the German extermination of Eastern European Jews
    D. launch a joint commercial venture in the oil-rich regions of the Middle East

29. Which of the following was NOT a factor in the 1920 victory of the Bolsheviks over White forces in the civil war?

    A. Support from several eastern European neighbors
    B. Control of most of the important railroad lines
    C. The refusal of the White forces to adopt a policy of land reforms
    D. Their success at creating an army

30. The United States Senate's ratification of the first international Non-Proliferation Treaty was postponed by the

    A. Tet offensive   B. Soviet invasion of Czechoslovakia
    C. Cuban missile crisis   D. Soviet invasion of Afghanistan

31. In 1917, after ten years of exile in Switzerland, Lenin arrived in Petrograd to radicalize the revolution. Which of the following enabled his re-entry into Russia?

    A. The fall of the tsar
    B. Aid from communist agents throughout eastern Europe who wanted to hasten the revolution
    C. Aid from the Germans, who wanted to see their Russian enemy weakened
    D. A formal call from the leaders of the Provisional Government

32. In what year was the Berlin Wall constructed? 32.____

    A. 1949 B. 1953 C. 1961 D. 1964

33. After the events of Bloody Sunday in 1905, Nicholas II established a system of consulta- 33.____
    tive representation to the people of Russia. The result of this was

    A. the loss of support from the armed forces
    B. the intensification of demands by protesters
    C. the first stable parliamentary structure in Russian history
    D. a temporary silencing of the revolutionary spirit

34. Which of the following events, in its illustration of the need for the free exchange of infor- 34.____
    mation, marked a turning point in Gorbachev's *glasnost* campaign?
    The

    A. 1985 Geneva Summit
    B. shooting down of KAL flight 007
    C. 1990 Central Committee meeting
    D. Chernobyl disaster

35. After the surrender of Japan to the United States in 1945, the Soviet Union was allowed 35.____
    each of the following EXCEPT

    A. a role in the postwar administration of Japan
    B. the occupation of Manchuria
    C. the occupation of all of Sakhalin Island
    D. the occupation of the Kuril Islands

36. Which of the following applied four times, and were denied, observer status at the 1990 36.____
    negotiations of the Conference on Security and Cooperation in Europe (CSCE)?

    A. Ukraine and Belorussia
    B. The trans-Caucasian republics
    C. Romania and Bulgaria
    D. The Baltic states

37. Which of the following best describes the communists' motivation for murdering Tsar 37.____
    Nicholas II and his family in July of 1918?

    A. The proximity of White army troops who might rally around the tsar
    B. The interests of tsarist World War I allies in the civil war
    C. A desire for revenge and justice
    D. Assurance that the monarchy could never be revived

38. Each of the following nations supplied troops to aid the 1968 Soviet invasion of Czecho- 38.____
    slovakia EXCEPT

    A. Poland B. East Germany
    C. Bulgaria D. Romania

39. During the era of the New Economic Policy, the foreign policy of the young Soviet nation was most clearly based on the principle that   39.___

    A. the success of the state would depend upon strict isolation and an adherence to the borders of the Soviet republics
    B. a brief and temporary period of peaceful co-existence with capitalist neighbors was the only way for the Soviet state to survive its initiation
    C. the only way to insure national security was to create a buffer zone of satellite states on the European front
    D. as long as capitalism and socialism existed, they could not live in peace

40. Toward the end of the Brezhnev era, the Soviet economy and society experienced a remarkable period of stagnation. The clearest cause of this was   40.___

    A. a decline in heavy industry
    B. the low turnover among aging Politburo members
    C. the growth of the younger segment of the population
    D. the degree of corruption at all government organizations

KEY (CORRECT ANSWERS)

1.	D	11.	C	21.	A	31.	C
2.	D	12.	D	22.	C	32.	C
3.	C	13.	C	23.	C	33.	B
4.	D	14.	C	24.	A	34.	D
5.	C	15.	D	25.	D	35.	A
6.	D	16.	A	26.	C	36.	D
7.	D	17.	B	27.	C	37.	A
8.	B	18.	B	28.	A	38.	D
9.	C	19.	B	29.	A	39.	D
10.	A	20.	D	30.	B	40.	B

TEST 3

DIRECTIONS: Each question or incomplete statement is followed by several suggested answers or completions. Select the one that BEST answers the question or completes the statement. *PRINT THE LETTER OF THE CORRECT ANSWER IN THE SPACE AT THE RIGHT.*

1. Which of the following was NOT generally a characteristic of revolutionary movements that arose in nineteenth-century Russia?

    A. An origin almost exclusively limited to the lower classes
    B. Ineffective organization
    C. General neglect of the cause of non-Russians against Tsarism
    D. Factionalism and unwillingness to compromise

    1.____

2. In the 1985 speech in which Gorbachev accepted his nomination as general secretary, he stated that the Soviet government's highest priorities would be

    A. economic revitalization and arms control
    B. *perestroika* and *glasnost*
    C. agricultural and educational reforms
    D. social reforms and a changing defense strategy

    2.____

3. After the Potsdam conference of 1945, the Allies seemed to be moving inevitably toward

    A. a sustained offensive against the Japanese mainland
    B. the cession of Eastern Europe to Soviet influence
    C. the occupation of Spain
    D. the partitioning of Germany

    3.____

4. Gorbachev unwittingly helped Yeltsin emerge as a competitor for power by

    A. allowing Eastern European reform movements to proceed unchallenged
    B. leaning to the right in his policies to accommodate conservatives
    C. enacting reforms too rapidly for the institutions to keep pace
    D. allowing price hikes on consumer items such as bread

    4.____

5. Under the terms of the NEP, Lenin and the Bolsheviks retained complete state control of

    A. banks   B. grain surpluses
    C. small factories   D. agricultural land

    5.____

6. Which of the following was a result of Krushchev's *Secret Speech* of February 1956? A(n)

    A. improvement in relations with the United States
    B. erosion of Krushchev's support in the Communist Party
    C. breakdown in Soviet control over parts of Eastern Europe
    D. improvement in relations with China

    6.____

7. During the 1840s, a number of revolutionary intellectual groups gained prominence in Russia. Which of the following was NOT one of these groups?

    A. Westerners   B. Populists
    C. Slavophiles   D. The Petrashevskists

    7.____

69

8. The last German offensive against Russia in the Second World War was launched in 1943 against the city of

   A. Harkov B. Stalingrad C. Kursk D. Smolensk

9. Which of the following quotas for Stalin's first Five-Year Plan was met in advance of the established deadline?

   A. Grain exports
   B. Consumer price stablization
   C. Employment index
   D. Coal production

10. Which of the following government organizations, under pressure from Gorbachev, made sweeping constitutional changes in 1990 including the popular election of the Soviet head of state?

    A. Central Committee
    B. Politburo
    C. Supreme Soviet
    D. Congress of People's Deputies

11. Which of the following best explains why Roosevelt and Churchill accepted the vagueness of Stalin's promises at the 1945 Yalta conference to establish democratically elected leadership in Eastern Europe?
    They

    A. did not discern the insincerity of Stalin's promise
    B. understood that the only way to dislodge the Soviets from these countries would be through a direct offensive
    C. wanted to hasten the onset of reconstruction in order to prevent further hostility in Western Europe
    D. perceived a desperate need for Russian involvement in the war with Japan

12. Which of the following Russia rulers, while being the first to openly discuss the issue of enserfment, established the institution of serfdom in the Ukraine?

    A. Peter the Great   B. Catherine the Great
    C. Nicholas I   D. Alexander III

13. During the administration of Yuri Andropov, his highest priority in the area of foreign relations was

    A. bringing an end to the quagmire in Afghanistan
    B. influencing a scaleback of the United States' MX intercontinental ballistic missile (ICBM) arsenal
    C. resolving the decades-old disputes with Japan over territorial boundaries
    D. attempting to prevent the NATO deployment of Pershing missiles throughout Western Europe

14. Who was the leader of the *right* faction of the Communist Party after Lenin's death?

    A. Zinoviev B. Kamenev C. Bukarin D. Stalin

15. Which of the following countries was the last to recognize the independence of the Baltic states from the former Soviet Union?

    A. Finland
    B. France
    C. Denmark
    D. United States

16. Which of the following Soviet cities was captured by the Germans during World War II?

    A. Stalingrad
    B. Leningrad
    C. Moscow
    D. Kiev

17. The main source of hard currency for the Soviet economy throughout most of the 1980s was

    A. arms exports
    B. oil exports
    C. tax revenues
    D. grain exports

18. Which of the following terms was used to describe post-emancipation serfs Russia who were tied to the village commune and the landlord's estate but who paid their dues to their owner?

    A. Obrok
    B. Barschina
    C. Household
    D. Kulak

19. Which of the following was NOT occupied by the Red Army when World War II ended in Europe?

    A. Hungary   B. Albania   C. Syria   D. Austria

20. The purpose of the 1957 Eisenhower Doctrine was to

    A. block Communist expansion in Southeast Asia
    B. prevent the construction of the Berlin Wall
    C. pave the way for improved East-West relations
    D. block Communist expansion in the Middle East

21. After the October Revolution, Lenin's efforts to bring all of Russia under Bolshevik authority centered on

    A. appeasement of the peasantry
    B. using the Red Army to put down opposition
    C. redistributing the lands of the nobility among the proletariat
    D. gaining control of the local soviets

22. Which of the following Eastern European countries had practiced democracy in its government prior to World War II?

    A. Czechoslovakia
    B. Hungary
    C. Yugoslavia
    D. Poland

23. What 1929 event did the most to render Stalin's power within the Communist Party unchallenged?

    A. Kirov's assassination
    B. The beginning of the first Five-Year Plan
    C. Trotsky's banishment from the Soviet Union
    D. The trial of Bukarin

24. In the 1960s, when it was clear that the United States was escalating its involvement in Vietnam, the Soviets' initial reaction was to

    A. urge the North Vietnamese to negotiate an end to the conflict
    B. establish a supply route to the North Vietnamese through China
    C. mobilize troops as a show of support for the North Vietnamese
    D. sit back and wait for China to become involved

25. After Gorbachev was overthrown in August of 1991, who assumed power as acting president?

    A. Valentin Pavlov B. Gennady Yanayev
    C. Boris Pugo   D. Yegor Ligachev

26. Who was the leader of the anticorruption drive that was undertaken in the latter part of the Brezhnev era?

    A. Mikhail Gorbachev B. Konstantin Chernenko
    C. Mikhail Suslov   D. Yuri Andropov

27. In the years after the Mongol conquest of Russia, the city of Moscow rose from a relatively minor city into the predominant political principality in Russia. Which of the following factors contributed to this?

    I. The collapse of the Mongol empire
    II. Territorial expansion by the Moscow princes
    III. The transference of the seat of the metropolitan of the Russian Church to Moscow
    IV. The political manipulations of Ivan I

    The CORRECT answer is:

    A. I only   B. II, III   C. IV only   D. II, III, IV

28. Each of the following was a desire expressed by Roosevelt and Churchill at the 1945 Yalta Conference EXCEPT

    A. Soviet participation in the war against Japan
    B. Soviet responsibility for the reconstruction of the Baltic states
    C. an agreement on the occupation of Germany
    D. Soviet guarantees of free elections in Eastern Europe

29. After taking power, the Bolsheviks undertook many actions which demonstrated their repudiation of democratic principles. The first indication occurred in 1917 when the party

    A. seized all private property
    B. established the Cheka, or political police
    C. outlawed strikes
    D. disbanded the first elected Constituent Assembly

30. Generally, the point at which the Soviet population came closest to losing its resolve during the German invasion that began in 1941 was when

    A. Stalingrad was all but destroyed
    B. the Germans laid siege to Leningrad
    C. the port of Odessa was lost
    D. government leaders fled Moscow

31. After the dissolution of the Soviet Union, the Communist Party was banned from activity in each of the following republics EXCEPT

    A. Estonia   B. Ukraine   C. Uzbekistan   D. Moldavia

32. The purpose of *shock workers* during Stalin's second Five-Year Plan was to

    A. put down strikes before they started
    B. raise production quotas
    C. secretly occupy and exploit leadership positions
    D. inform on other workers who were lazy or agitators

33. At the 19th Communist Party Congress in 1952, the Politburo was transformed into an organization known as the

    A. MGB   B. Presidium   C. Cominform   D. KGB

34. The most significant reason for the failure of the student-sponsored revolutionary movement of the 1870s was that

    A. Alexander II's reform programs silenced many protesters
    B. the tsar's intelligence agents were able to anticipate and prevent many of their activities
    C. the movement was extremely nationalistic and excluded many groups who could have added power to the revolt
    D. the students took their protests directly to rural peasants who were suspicious of their motives

35. In the midst of his campaign against the Soviets, Hitler discovered that his offensive would not be a blitzkrieg but a protracted conflict. The primary reason for the slow progress was

    A. the intense cold of the eastern climate
    B. the diversion of German troops to the western front in France
    C. difficulty in maintaining supply lines
    D. lack of personnel

36. Throughout the 1920s, the efforts of the Soviet Union's Comintern were focused on each of the following countries EXCEPT

    A. China   B. Great Britain
    C. the United States D. Germany

37. The widespread ethnic deportations ordered by Stalin in the 1940s displaced minorities from each of the following groups EXCEPT

    A. Mongols   B. Turks   C. Jews   D. Caucasian

38. Who was the initial leader of the Provisional Government that was established after the March Revolution of 1917?

    A. Prince Georgii Lvov   B. Lenin
    C. Trotsky   D. Aleksandr Kerensky

39. In 1991, as some of the former Soviet republics were considering their reconstitution into a confederacy, many leaders, including Yeltsin and Gorbachev, considered the key to these arrangements to be persuading _____ to sign a confederating treaty.

    A. the Central Asian states
    B. the trans-Caucasian states
    C. the Baltic states
    D. Ukraine

40. Which of the following was a result of the second general purge undertaken by the Communist Party in 1929?

    A. An increasing division between the left and right factions
    B. The recall of many foreign diplomats
    C. Highly vocal protests undertaken by the urban workers
    D. The flight of highly placed officials

KEY (CORRECT ANSWERS)

1.	A	11.	B	21.	D	31.	C
2.	A	12.	B	22.	A	32.	B
3.	D	13.	D	23.	C	33.	B
4.	B	14.	C	24.	A	34.	D
5.	A	15.	A	25.	B	35.	C
6.	C	16.	D	26.	D	36.	C
7.	B	17.	B	27.	D	37.	C
8.	C	18.	A	28.	B	38.	A
9.	C	19.	C	29.	D	39.	D
10.	A	20.	D	30.	D	40.	D

TEST 4

DIRECTIONS: Each question or incomplete statement is followed by several suggested answers or completions. Select the one that BEST answers the question or completes the statement. *PRINT THE LETTER OF THE CORRECT ANSWER IN THE SPACE AT THE RIGHT.*

1. The *Communist bourgeoisie*, a sub-class of conspicuous consumers, reached its peak under the government of

    A. Stalin B. Krushchev C. Brezhnev D. Andropov

    1.____

2. Which of the following were demands made by strikers during the Revolution of 1905?
    I. A constituent assembly
    II. Freedom of the press, speech, and assembly
    III. An 8-hour work day
    IV. Universal suffrage
    The CORRECT answer is:

    A. I, IV B. I, II, III C. II *only* D. III, IV

    2.____

3. In 1982, United States Secretary of State George Shultz outlined a set of conditions which the Soviet Union would be required to meet in order to establish better East-West relations. Which of the following was NOT one of these conditions?

    A. North Vietnamese withdrawal from Cambodia
    B. Relaxed tensions in Poland
    C. Withdrawal of intermediate-range SS-20 missiles aimed at Western Europe targets
    D. Soviet withdrawal from Afghanistan

    3.____

4. Josef Stalin's view of the Communist party in the 1920s can best be described as a

    A. temporary but necessary evil that would lay the groundwork for stability
    B. conquering army in an occupied country
    C. semi-democratic vehicle for the limited exchange of ideas
    D. benevolent patron among the benighted masses

    4.____

5. An important difference in the foreign policy of Krushchev from that of Lenin and Stalin was that Krushchev

    A. acknowledged some benefits of capitalism
    B. repudiated the goal of world revolution
    C. aggressively professed the desire for world domination
    D. recognized the concept of neutrality

    5.____

6. What was the term for the elite legislative branch of the Soviet government?

    A. Congress of People's Deputies B. Supreme Soviet
    C. Council of Ministers D. Soviet of the Union

    6.____

7. Which of the Soviet republics, in 1990, rejected declarations of sovereignty by the Abkhaz Autonomous Republic and the South Ossetian Autonomous Region?

    A. Georgia B. Moldavia C. Tajikistan D. Armenia

    7.____

8. In the period from 1913-1914, which of the following happened FIRST?

    A. Germany declared war on Russia and France
    B. Serbia and Bulgaria declared war on each other
    C. Britain declared war on Austria-Hungary and Germany
    D. Austria-Hungary declared war on Serbia

9. Approximately what percentage of Leningrad's population died during the German siege that lasted from 1941-1944?

    A. 10   B. 25   C. 35   D. 50

10. The anti-Bolshevik unrest that followed the civil war in Russia reached its climax in 1921 with

    A. July Days   B. the Kornilov affair
    C. Bloody Sunday   D. the Kronstadt rebellion

11. Which of the following issues was NOT on the agenda of the 1955 Geneva summit?

    A. Recognition of Communist China
    B. German reunification
    C. Improvement of East-West relations
    D. European security

12. Which of the following was most clearly accomplished by the Stalin government's first Five-Year Plan?

    A. An adequate if not abundant amount of available manufactured goods
    B. The completion of several large industrial projects
    C. An increase in real wages
    D. An increase in the buying power of the ruble

13. The purpose of the 1968 Brezhnev Doctrine was to

    A. settle once and for all the differences in Soviet and Chinese communist ideology
    B. warn the United States and other Western powers against subversive activity in other communist states
    C. confirm the enduring Soviet commitment to the principle of world revolution
    D. justify Soviet interference in the affairs of other communist states

14. In what year were the Russian peasants finally emancipated from enserfment?

    A. 1796   B. 1856   C. 1861   D. 1888

15. By the middle of 1965, relations between the United States and the Soviet Union had once again become strained, this time because of

    A. the escalation of United States involvement in the Vietnam conflict
    B. the Soviets' overtures to France, which had just withdrawn from NATO
    C. the deliberately slow pace at which Soviet missiles were being dismantled in Cuba
    D. Soviet involvement in the India-Pakistan conflict

16. Each of the following factors led the Allies to advocate the overthrow of the Bolsheviks in Russia after the conclusion of World War I EXCEPT

    A. the desire to re-establish an eastern line of defense against German and Austrian aggression
    B. the Bolsheviks' ambition to seize territory in Eastern Europe
    C. anticapitalist propaganda
    D. the Bolsheviks' disavowal of previous foreign debts

17. Which of the following was added to the Union of Soviet Socialist Republics in 1929?

    A. Ukraine
    B. Lithuania
    C. Turkemenistan
    D. Belorussia

18. Which of the following Soviet Socialist Republics was created by Stalin at the close of World War II, largely from land seized from Romania?

    A. Tajikistan
    B. Moldavia
    C. Bukovina
    D. Bessarabia

19. Which of the following organizations was considered to be the ideological nerve center of the Communist Party in the years following World War II?

    A. NKVP
    B. Agitprop
    C. Cominform
    D. Politburo

20. Which of the following factors contributed to the Bolsheviks' ability to remain in power after the October Revolution?
    I. An outreach to the aristocracy for token policy advice
    II. A type of tatalitarianism that eliminated dissent and challenges
    III. Appropriation of the popular policies of their opponents
    IV. Better overall organization than their rivals

    The CORRECT answer is:

    A. I, III
    B. I, II, IV
    C. II, III, IV
    D. IV *only*

21. The *turning point* in the war between Germany and Russia that began in 1941, after which the Germans were mostly on the retreat, was the

    A. battle of Stalingrad
    B. siege of Leningrad
    C. battle of Moscow
    D. battle of Kursk

22. Which of the following best describes the effect of the Soviet government's New Economic Policy on the membership of the Communist party?
    A(n)

    A. disillusionment with the leaders of the party and an alienation from Communist ideals
    B. understanding of Bolshevism as a temporary phase on the way to national maturity
    C. surge of nationalistic pride
    D. realization of the practicalities of converting a revolutionary movement into a government

23. In the initial post-World War II period, each of the following countries had a genuine friendship with the Soviet Union EXCEPT

    A. Czechoslovakia
    B. Romania
    C. Bulgaria
    D. Yugoslavia

24. In Stalin's appeal to the Soviet people after the German invasion, he was successful in rallying them mostly because

    A. he reminded them of the principles of their founder, Lenin, and denounced the invasion as an intolerable obstacle on the road to socialism
    B. he appealed to their devotion to Mother Russia and eased restrictions on the church
    C. they knew most would be conscripted into the war effort anyway
    D. he related frightening tales of German atrocities

25. The *Decembrists* can best be described as

    A. rural peasants led in a revolt against the rule of Catherine the Great
    B. aristocratic advocates of a constitutional monarchy who attempted to seize power after the death of Alexander I
    C. Utopian socialists who agitated against the rule of Nicholas I
    D. a group of proletarians who were more moderate than the Octobrists in their revolutionary zeal

26. For what reason was nothing done by Stalin's government to bring relief to the sufferers of the 1932-1933 famine?

    A. The government was unwilling to give up the grain exports that were helping to finance the Five-Year Plan.
    B. The government considered the famine a political weapon that would break the peasants' will.
    C. There was simply not enough food available to the government to be of any assistance to the peasants.
    D. The government was unaware of the extent of the famine.

27. Which of the following is true of the Nepmen, the class of capitalists created by the New Economic Policy?

    A. Their children were given scholarships at the university level.
    B. They were members of professional associations.
    C. They were mostly speculators.
    D. They were enfranchised.

28. Which of the following events allowed the Soviets to concentrate their troops along the European front in 1941?

    A. The secret protocol of the 1939 non-aggression pact with Germany
    B. A non-aggression pact with Japan
    C. Agreements made with Great Britain and the United States in Tehran
    D. A victory over Japan in Mongolia

29. For what reason did the Bolsheviks move the Russian capital to Moscow in March of 1918?

   A. Petrograd offered too many reminders of the tsar's rule.
   B. Lenin's family roots were in Moscow.
   C. Moscow was more easily defensible against military or counter-revolutionary attacks.
   D. Moscow had better access to the Black Sea trade route.

30. The May 1960 Soviet-American summit was canceled because of the

   A. Suez crisis
   B. Cuban missile crisis
   C. U-2 incident
   D. construction of the Berlin Wall

31. The *changing landmarks* movement of the 1920s was embraced mostly by

   A. middle peasants who were profiting by the New Economic Policy
   B. exiled sympathizers of the monarchy
   C. urban laborers
   D. right-wing conservatives in the Russian intelligentsia

32. Just prior to World War II, the educational theories proposed by Makarenko became the official theories of Soviet education. According to Makarenko, the institutions which provided the model context for teaching children were the

   A. government and the church
   B. hospital and the sanitarium
   C. church and the family
   D. army and the labor colony

33. The event which most clearly brought an end to the detente process between the United States and the Soviet Union was the

   A. Soviet invasion of Czechoslovakia
   B. demise of the 1972 trade accord
   C. Soviet invasion of Afghanistan
   D. United States deployment of Pershing missiles throughout Western Europe

34. Which of the following were characteristics of the Russian economy from the period of 1880-1900?
   I. The rapid expansion of the railways
   II. A flourishing spirit of capitalism and entrepreneur-ship
   III. Moderate reforms in labor laws
   IV. An influx of foreign capital

   The CORRECT answer is:

   A. I, IV   B. I, III, IV   C. II, III   D. II, III, IV

35. At the time of the Soviet Union's collapse, which of the following republican capital cities had the lowest percentage of ethnic Russians in its population?

   A. Baku, Azerbaijan
   B. Alma-Ata, Kazakhstan
   C. Yerevan, Armenia
   D. Tblisi, Georgia

36. Under the New Economic Policy, approximately what percentage of the country's wholesale trade was conducted by the state?

   A. 8   B. 15   C. 45   D. 75

37. The result of the 1943 discovery of secret grave sites at Katyn, near Smolensk, was the

   A. recognition by the Allies that Jews were being exterminated by the Germans
   B. aggravation of hostilities between Poles and Russians
   C. Allies' granting of Russian annexation of much of eastern Poland
   D. initiation of the Nuremberg trials

38. Which of the following Soviet agencies, founded in 1921, was responsible for charting the nation's economic course?

   A. SEC   B. Orgburo   C. COMECON   D. Gosplan

39. Which of the following was NOT a member of the Warsaw Pact?

   A. Bulgaria
   B. Hungary
   C. Yugoslavia
   D. Czechoslovakia

40. Which of the following was not a member of the Central Treaty Organization (CENTO)?

   A. Pakistan   B. Turkey   C. Lebanon   D. Iran

KEY (CORRECT ANSWERS)

1. C	11. A	21. A	31. D
2. B	12. B	22. A	32. D
3. C	13. D	23. B	33. C
4. B	14. C	24. B	34. B
5. D	15. A	25. B	35. C
6. B	16. A	26. B	36. D
7. A	17. C	27. C	37. B
8. B	18. B	28. B	38. D
9. D	19. B	29. C	39. C
10. D	20. C	30. C	40. C

EXAMINATION SECTION
TEST 1

DIRECTIONS: Each question or incomplete statement is followed by several suggested answers or completions. Select the one that BEST answers the question or completes the statement. *PRINT THE LETTER OF THE CORRECT ANSWER IN THE SPACE AT THE RIGHT.*

1. In 1930, when Stalin temporarily retreated from his policy of collectivization, he

    A. called upon the peasants to voluntarily increase production
    B. blamed its failure on the local party activists
    C. began to devise a more efficient means of controlling the farms
    D. announced a resumption of the tax in kind provisions of the New Economic Policy

    1._____

2. The most significant result of the *tax in kind* provision of the New Economic Policy regarding agricultural production was that it

    A. gave the government a greater span of control over the distribution of agricultural products
    B. reduced the overall tax burden on the peasantry
    C. limited the amount of grain exports that could be undertaken by the state
    D. limited arbitrary action by the state regarding the disposition of agricultural surpluses

    2._____

3. One of the results of the Potsdam Conference of 1945 was to tacitly establish a fifth, _____ occupation zone in Germany.

    A. Dutch   B. Czechoslovakian
    C. Polish   D. Canadian

    3._____

4. Of all the decisions which reflected badly on the post-revolutionary Provisional Government, the one which did the most to bring the government down was to

    A. delay land redistribution until a legislature could be elected
    B. guarantee free speech, assembly, press, and religion
    C. continue the war effort despite the people's lack of support
    D. mandate changes in local governments

    4._____

5. The post-World War II Communist Information Bureau, or Cominform, suffered an early setback when

    A. the Red Army invaded Czechoslovakia
    B. the Allies carried out the Berlin airlift
    C. the Yugoslav leader Tito broke with Moscow
    D. Austria was liberated on the condition of neutrality

    5._____

6. Stalin's Five-Year Plans eventually took on a form that differed greatly from the tenets of Bolshevism, The most striking example of this was the

    A. use of terror to put down opposition
    B. use of forced labor as a punishment for party disloyalty
    C. exclusion of priests from participation in any sector of society
    D. use of material incentives to stimulate production

    6._____

7. The nationalist feelings during the latter half of the nineteenth century had generally not escalated to the point of separatism. In particular, a sense of religious solidarity between _____ seemed to set limits to the animosity between the two groups.

    A. Russians and Ukrainians
    B. Poles and Russians
    C. Baltic Germans and Poles
    D. Jews and Slavs

8. The driving force behind the failed coup against Gorbachev's government in 1991 were

    A. fiscal conservatives who believed an economic collapse was imminent
    B. laborers who could not imagine surviving the coming wave of price hikes
    C. liberals who supported Boris Yeltsin
    D. right-wing conservatives who did not want to see the end of the union

9. The power struggle among Bolsheviks during the era of the New Economic Policy can best be described as a struggle between

    A. isolationists and proponents of world revolution
    B. supporters of Stalin and supporters of Lenin
    C. loyalists to the ideals of the party and loyalists to the actions of the top party leaders
    D. those who advocated an immediate conversion to communism and those who believed in a more gradual, orderly process

10. In 1955, the Kremlin withdrew its military forces from the nation of

    A. Bulgaria
    B. East Germany
    C. Austria
    D. Syria

11. The primary focus of Stalin's first Five-Year Plan was the

    A. financing of industrial projects through agricultural production
    B. elevation of the peasant to the Soviet middle class
    C. updating and advancement of the Soviet armament
    D. elimination of the kulaks

12. Under Gorbachev's concept of *perestroika*, the acceleration of social and economic development were to be accomplished in the long run by

    A. reduced alcholism
    B. technological modernization
    C. greater worker efficiency
    D. reduced corruption

13. In a Soviet republic, an administrative area equivalent to a city district was known as a(n)

    A. raion   B. adjutant   C. tikhon   D. oblast

14. After the Bolsheviks seized power in 1917, the Council of People's Commissars was established as the highest ruling body in the country. Which of the following was assigned responsibility for handling the desires and complaints of national minority groups?

    A. V. I. Lenin
    B. Lev Kamenev
    C. Leon Trotsky
    D. Josef Stalin

15. During the rule of the early Romanovs, the most important development in foreign relations was probably

    A. continued westward expansion into the area now known as the Ukraine
    B. the normalization of relations with Prussia
    C. the acquisition of territory on the Gulf of Finland's shores in conflicts with the Swedish Empire
    D. the fortification of the eastern frontier against further threats of invasion

16. Generally, the reason that Gorbachev began to lose his hold on power in the late 1980s was because

    A. he had been unsuccessful in weeding his enemies out of the party structure
    B. the pace of his reforms was considered by most Soviet citizens to be too fast
    C. of the rise of the populist hero Boris Yeltsin
    D. the legislature he had created was gaining in influence

17. The industrial elements of the government's New Economic Policy had an adverse effect on

    A. the stability of the currency
    B. labor productivity
    C. agricultural production
    D. the employment rate

18. The Chinese territory of Manchuria was considered to be important to the Soviets in the late 1930s because it

    A. was home to several Soviet-controlled seaports
    B. contained the railway to Vladivostok
    C. was virtually a Soviet protectorate
    D. was an important staging ground for defensive movements against Japanese aggression

19. After the Allies had lifted their blockade of the Soviet Union in 1920, the government agreed upon terms proposed by the British. Which of the following was NOT one of these terms?

    A. Repatriation of prisoners of war
    B. Bilateral access to agricultural exports
    C. An end to propaganda warfare
    D. Recognition in principle of debts to private individuals

20. Which of the following was the reform-minded party secretary who advocated the development of *democratic socialism* in Czechoslovakia in the 1960s?

    A. Gustav Husak
    B. Vaclav Havel
    C. Imre Nagy
    D. Alexander Dubcek

21. Russia's first two Dumas (1906-1907) can most effectively be characterized as legislative assemblies that

    A. accomplished a series of land and education reforms before being dissolved by Prime Minister Stolypin
    B. were too liberal to cooperate with the government and were promptly dissolved
    C. directly representative bodies with unrestricted member franchisement
    D. accomplished little because of the lack of coherent rules of order

22. Which of the following republics was among the last to joint the Commonwealth of Independent States (CIS)?

    A. Georgia   B. Azerbaijan   C. Belorussia   D. Ukraine

23. During the era of the New Economic Policy, the poorest Soviet citizens were generally the

    A. workers   B. Nepmen   C. intellectuals   D. peasants

24. After rising to power, Brezhnev advocated two *first priorities* in the Soviet government's resource allocation. These were

    A. heavy industry and consumer goods
    B. agriculture and foreign intelligence
    C. the military and agriculture
    D. consumer goods and services

25. Which of the following was NOT an element of the Bolsheviks' policy of War Communism, adopted in 1918?
    The

    A. redistribution of land
    B. outlawing of strikes
    C. repudiation of the tsar's foreign debts
    D. elimination of markets

26. The first *soviet* in Russian history was formed in St. Petersburg in

    A. 1865 in response to the emancipation of the serfs
    B. 1905 during the October strike
    C. 1914 in response to the declaration of war
    D. 1917 after the monarchy had fallen

27. The Russian Social Democratic movement, which arose in the nineteenth century, had its roots in the *Osvobashdenie truda* (Liberation of Labor), an organization founded by

    A. Nikolai Chernyshevsky   B. Leon Trotsky
    C. Julius Martov   D. George Plekhanov

28. The moderate faction of the People's Democratic Party of Afghanistan, which was formed in 1965 and lost control over the Afghani government just prior to the Soviets' 1979 intervention, was the

    A. parcham   B. hezbollah   C. khalq   D. mujahidin

29. Which of the following were elements of the marriage code adopted by the Soviet government in 1928?

    I. Both civil and religious marriages were equally valid,
    II. Either husband or wife could dissolve a marriage, without necessarily informing the other.
    III. The illegal concept of illegitimacy pertaining to children was abolished.
    IV. Both registered and unregistered marriages were equally valid.

    The CORRECT answer is:

    A. I, IV   B. I, II, III
    C. II, III   D. I, II, III, IV

30. The effect of World War II on Soviet foreign policy could best be described as a concept of security that involved

    A. military superiority and a determination to fight offensive wars on enemy soil
    B. the rapid achievement of economic superiority and a retrenchment of Soviet borders
    C. the expansion of the Soviet empire and a focus on deterrence
    D. reaching out to defend the interests of ethnic Russian minorities in other countries

31. Which of the following was the term for the direct popular ballots, held in the late 1980s and early 1990s, in which citizens of the Soviet republics decided political issues such as independence?

    A. Co-options
    B. Plebiscites
    C. Prosceniums
    D. Referendums

32. During the India/Pakistan war of 1971, Russia offered military aid to India. Which of the following countries supported Pakistan?

    A. France
    B. The People's Republic of China
    C. Great Britain
    D. The United States

33. At the 1943 meeting between Stalin, Churchill, and Roosevelt in Tehran, the most important issue for Stalin was

    A. the establishment of a western European front
    B. the post-war status of Germany
    C. a role in reconstruction
    D. the post-war status of Poland

34. In 1956, Communist Party control suffered a temporary breakdown in the nations of

    A. Romania and Bulgaria
    B. Poland and Hungary
    C. Bulgaria and Albania
    D. Yugoslavia and Czechoslovakia

35. Which of the following was NOT an industrial component of the NEP?

    A. Allowance of foreigners to lease factories
    B. The application of self-financing to forced labor camps
    C. Authorization of small private businesses
    D. Privatization of major transport sectors

36. From 1934-1936, Russian history underwent a dramatic change at the hands of Stalin. Which of the following best describes what it had become?

    A. Indiscriminate and rambling
    B. Mythologized and inclusive
    C. Nationalized and relativized
    D. Cold and empirical

37. Which of the following were major concerns of Peter the Great (1682-1725)?
    I. Putting down revolutionary movements begun by the landed classes
    II. Fighting Sweden for the Baltic territories
    III. Modernizing the country along Western lines
    IV. Improving conditions for the peasantry
    The CORRECT answer is:

    A. I, IV
    B. II, III
    C. I, II, III
    D. II, III, IV

38. In the early years of his administration, the strongest resistance to Gorbachev's domestic reforms came from

    A. laborers
    B. the lower levels of the bureaucracies
    C. enterprise managers
    D. upper-level party officials

39. To proponents of the *changing landmarks* movement of the 1920s, the New Economic Policy was an indication of

    A. the inevitable decline of Bolshevism
    B. the strength of counterrevolutionary elements throughout Russia
    C. a victory of idealism over pragmatism
    D. a revived revolutionary movement

40. Throughout the Soviet era, the plenum of the CPSU's Central Committee was held at LEAST _____ a year.

    A. once
    B. twice
    C. three times
    D. four times

KEY (CORRECT ANSWERS)

1. B	11. A	21. B	31. B
2. D	12. B	22. B	32. B
3. C	13. A	23. A	33. A
4. C	14. D	24. C	34. B
5. C	15. A	25. A	35. D
6. D	16. D	26. B	36. C
7. A	17. D	27. D	37. B
8. D	18. B	28. A	38. B
9. C	19. B	29. C	39. A
10. C	20. D	30. A	40. B

TEST 2

DIRECTIONS: Each question or incomplete statement is followed by several suggested answers or completions. Select the one that BEST answers the question or completes the statement. *PRINT THE LETTER OF THE CORRECT ANSWER IN THE SPACE AT THE RIGHT.*

1. After the Bolshevik seizure of power in 1917, legislative authority was in practice exercised mostly by the

    A. All-Russian Congress of Soviets
    B. Central Executive Committee
    C. Red Army
    D. Council of People's Commissars and the Council of Workers' and Peasants' Defense

    1.____

2. Article 6 of the Soviet constitution, which had guaranteed the Communist party's leading role in society, was first revoked in the year

    A. 1956 B. 1985 C. 1988 D. 1990

    2.____

3. The most significant flaw with the first Five-Year Plan enacted by Stalin was

    A. an imbalance between the pace of enterprises and resources such as raw materials and labor
    B. an emphasis on the military and defense elements at the expense of infrastructure
    C. its insistent refusal to consider outside assistance
    D. a focus on the processes involved in industry, rather than the products themselves

    3.____

4. The Soviet Union did not veto the 1950 United Nations resolution condemning the North Korean invasion and authorizing military intervention because it

    A. wanted to maintain the pretense that it had known nothing of the invasion in advance
    B. was still exercising caution in light of Eisenhower's overt nuclear threats
    C. wanted to draw the western powers into an armed conflict in Asia
    D. was boycotting the Security Council over the U.N.'s exclusion of communist China

    4.____

5. The new legislative body created by Gorbachev in 1988 was the

    A. Soviet of Nationalities
    B. Supreme Soviet
    C. Congress of People's Deputies
    D. Emergency Committee

    5.____

6. Implementation of the 1972 trade agreement between the United States and the Soviet Union hinged on congressional approval of most-favored-nation (MFN) status for Soviet production. The congressional debate over this issue focused on

    A. the Soviets' emigration policies toward Jews
    B. the Soviets' expansionist foreign policy
    C. international anti-dumping restrictions
    D. nuclear proliferation

    6.____

7. When the political alliance between Stalin and Bukarin became strained in the late 1920s, it was over the issue of

    A. government centralization
    B. the role of the Comintern
    C. collectivization
    D. food-supplies policy

8. Gorbachev's *new thinking (novoe myshlenie)* policy embraced changes in the way the Soviet Union thought about

    A. economic stimulation
    B. defense
    C. the relationship of church and state
    D. civil rights

9. Most pragmatic Communists viewed the Bolshevik government's New Economic Policy as

    A. the only real way for productivity to increase
    B. a necessary evil for staying in power
    C. a strategic feint that would invite foreign investment
    D. an outright betrayal of party principles

10. In the period immediately following World War II, the heir apparent to Stalin in the Communist Party structure was widely regarded to be

    A. A. A. Zhdanov
    B. Georgi Malenkov
    C. Nikita Krushchev
    D. Vyacheslav Molotov

11. The _____ contributed the most to the growth of a proletarian class in Russia's cities at the turn of the century.

    A. overall increase in the nation's population
    B. collapse of the communal system of agriculture
    C. reformation of Russia's educational system
    D. rapid rate of industrialization

12. In which Russian city did industrialists gain most from the World War I effort?

    A. Vladivostok
    B. Moscow
    C. Odessa
    D. Petrograd (St. Petersburg)

13. During the implementation of his collectivization policy, Stalin's first efforts at breaking the kulaks involved

    A. army units
    B. the poorest peasants
    C. the GPU
    D. local police

14. Which of the following best explains why Konstantin Chernenko was chosen to succeed Yiri Andropov after Andropov's 1984 death?

    A. He was likely to function as a stable transitional leader.
    B. His cordial personality drew in and secured the allegiances of party members with widely differing agendas.
    C. He was the party member most likely to slow down the pace of Andropov's reforms.
    D. He was an intellectual who could debate strongly questions of domestic and foreign policy.

15. In 1929 the Transcaucasian republic of the U.S.S.R. was divided into its component parts. Which was NOT one of these republics?

    A. Georgia
    B. Azerbaijan
    C. Uzbekistan
    D. Armenia

    15.____

16. At the Yalta summit, Stalin's argument for a dominant Soviet role in postwar Eastern Europe was based on the

    A. fact that the Soviets had fought the Germans and suffered devastating losses long before the Allies established a European front
    B. ease with which lines of supply and control could be established through the western and southern Soviet cities
    C. cultural and political ties that the Soviet Union already shared with the ethnic populations of Eastern European territories
    D. fact that the Soviets already occupied these areas

    16.____

17. Which of the following Soviet satellite states publicly criticized the 1968 invasion of Czechoslovakia?

    A. Bulgaria
    B. Hungary
    C. Albania
    D. Yugoslavia

    17.____

18. In general, the mainland Chinese government tended to view the Soviet Union under Krushchev as a(n)

    A. persistent and untrustworthy threat to the integrity of the northwestern border
    B. betrayal of the socialist principles upon which the two nations had been founded
    C. patron nation that would enable its own rise to prominence
    D. unstable and unpredictable foreign policy machine

    18.____

19. Among the following, which country was the last to recognize the Soviet Republic in 1924?

    A. Italy
    B. China
    C. France
    D. Austria

    19.____

20. Which of the following parties won a majority in the Constituent Assembly elected after the October Revolution of 1917?
    The

    A. Kadets
    B. Socialist Revolutionaries
    C. Mensheviks
    D. Communists (Bolsheviks)

    20.____

21. The paradox that came to be associated with Gorbachev's *perestroika* reforms was that

    A. the more conciliatory the Soviet Union became in foreign policy, the more suspicious its Western negotiating partners became
    B. the more past abuses by government officials and programs were discovered, the angrier and more disgusted the population became with the present government
    C. prosperity was impossible without changes, but the population's willingness to accept change depended on a better standard of living
    D. the more *open* Soviet society became, the more the stability of the administration was threatened

    21.____

22. Which of the following events sparked the inception of the *Great Terror* begun by Stalin in 1934?

    A. A devastating famine
    B. The Kirov assassination
    C. The Shakhty trial
    D. The Kronstadt Rebellion

23. The most important domestic aspect of Krushchev's *de-Stalination* process was

    A. granting greater freedom of movement within the Soviet Union
    B. operating government organizations during regular business hours
    C. the repudiation of terror
    D. the relaxation of labor discipline

24. The Kadets, a party created in 1905, were composed mostly of

    A. radicals from the laboring class
    B. moderates from the nobility
    C. liberals from the rural peasantry
    D. liberals from the rising professional class

25. Throughout the 1920s, the poorest and weakest of the Soviet republics was

    A. Armenia   B. Bikhara   C. Belorussia   D. Azerbaijan

26. The chief irony of Soviet foreign policy during the 1920s and 1930s was that

    A. Russia's initial support of the Nazis in Germany was due to a desire for the spread of communism there
    B. while the Soviets worked for the eventual demise of capitalism, Moscow actively courted foreign investment in the Five-Year Plans
    C. all of its diplomatic relations were aimed entirely at Soviet security
    D. while it was looking to strengthen its borders to the west, China was advancing from the east

27. The worst labor unrest in the USSR since the 1920s occurred in July 1989 when _____ throughout much of the country went on strike to express their opposition to the government.

    A. coal miners
    B. steel workers
    C. farm laborers
    D. transit workers

28. During Stalin's implementation of *dekulakization* of the peasant class, approximately how many poor peasants were deported for every kulak?

    A. 1   B. 3   C. 5   D. 9

29. The domestic program that probably did the most to damage Krushchev's standing among Soviet leaders was the

    A. decentralization of economic planning power
    B. government reorganization into a *bifurcated* structure
    C. Virgin Lands agricultural initiative
    D. social reforms of de-Stalinization

30. In the disaffected Soviet citizenry of the late Brezhnev era, the most alienated members of Soviet society tended to be

    A. intellectuals
    B. youth
    C. laborers
    D. lower-level party bureaucrats

31. In the 1980s, the People's Republic of China claimed *three obstacles* that stood in the way of normalized Sino-Soviet relations. Which of the following was NOT one of these? The

    A. Soviet occupation of Afghanistan
    B. lack of reparations made to families of the downed KAL commercial airliner
    C. North Vietnamese occupation of Cambodia
    D. presence of Soviet troops along the Russian-Chinese border

32. The primary means by which Stalin stimulated enthusiasm for his first Five-Year Plan was

    A. the establishment of financial incentives for the manager of individual projects
    B. the publication of projected *control figures*
    C. the public offer of urban employment to peasants
    D. purging the program's opponents from the government

33. By 1986, the only real dramatic changes undertaken by the Gorbachev administration had occurred in the area of

    A. agricultural reforms   B. personnel
    C. arms reduction   D. social reforms

34. The issue over which Lenin and Stalin had their falling out in the early 1920s was the

    A. elements of the New Economic Policy
    B. status of Russian Jews
    C. successor to Lenin in the government
    D. autonomy of the other Soviet republics

35. Which of the following groups was a Caucasian minority within the Soviet Union?

    A. Kalmyks   B. Chechens   C. Balkars   D. Tatars

36. In the early 1930s, Stalin's policy toward the German Hitler regime was shaped by each of the following factors EXCEPT

    A. the fear of seeing the Communists coming to power and building a more successful state in Germany
    B. the conviction that the Nazis were nationalists who were opposed to the Versailles system
    C. a fear of seeing capitalism become firmly established in Germany
    D. a hatred of the Social Democrats

37. In 1946, under intense Western pressure, the Soviet Union withdrew its forces from the nation of   37._____

    A. Turkey
    B. Iran
    C. Austria
    D. Czechoslovakia

38. Which of the following is considered to be the *father of Russian Marxism?*   38._____

    A. Plekhanov   B. Martov   C. Bakunin   D. Lenin

39. The Foreign Minister announced his resignation from the Soviet government in December 1990 because he   39._____

    A. could not reconcile his beliefs with the reforms enacted by Gorbachev
    B. was to become the leader of a newly independent Georgian republic
    C. wanted to position himself for a place in Yeltsin's government
    D. feared that a dictatorship was approaching

40. The initial motivation for Stalin's collectivization policy in the late 1920s was   40._____

    A. tighter government control of agricultural resources
    B. the elimination of the kulaks
    C. to ward off another food crisis by making distribution more efficient
    D. increased agricultural production

KEY (CORRECT ANSWERS)

1. D	11. D	21. C	31. B
2. D	12. D	22. B	32. B
3. A	13. B	23. C	33. B
4. D	14. A	24. D	34. D
5. C	15. C	25. D	35. B
6. A	16. A	26. B	36. C
7. D	17. D	27. A	37. B
8. B	18. B	28. B	38. A
9. B	19. C	29. B	39. D
10. A	20. B	30. B	40. D

TEST 3

DIRECTIONS: Each question or incomplete statement is followed by several suggested answers or completions. Select the one that BEST answers the question or completes the statement. *PRINT THE LETTER OF THE CORRECT ANSWER IN THE SPACE AT THE RIGHT.*

1. After the 1979 meeting between Jimmy Carter and Leonid Brezhnev, the next meeting between a United States president and a Soviet leader occurred between

    A. Reagan and Andropov
    B. Reagan and Gorbachev
    C. Bush and Gorbachev
    D. Clinton and Yeltsin

2. From the first day of the 1917 revolution, Lenin perceived the main enemy of the proletariat to be

    A. the Russian Orthodox church
    B. Jews
    C. the intelligentsia
    D. factory owners

3. In the spring of 1991, the Soviet government held a referendum on whether the Soviet Union should be preserved as a *renewed federation of equal sovereign republics.* Each of the following republics participated in this referendum EXCEPT

    A. Armenia
    B. Kazakhstan
    C. Azerbaijan
    D. Ukraine

4. Which of the following was a result of the Decembrist revolt of 1825?

    A. The splintering of the Decembrists into several revolutionary movements
    B. A series of token reforms that satisfied very few revolutionaries
    C. The eventual emancipation of Russian serfs
    D. A new era of repression under the new emperor

5. The significance of the battle of Kursk, fought by the Germans and Russians in 1943, was that it

    A. enabled the Russian march to within 60 miles of Warsaw
    B. shattered the myth that the Germans were invincible in warm weather
    C. virtually destroyed the German air force
    D. was the largest infantry battle ever fought

6. In which of the following ways did the famine of 1932-1933 in the Soviet Union differ from the famine of 1921-22?
    I. The 1932-33 famine covered a smaller geographic area.
    II. It moved the government to request outside assistance.
    III. It killed a larger number of people.
    IV. It necessitated an end to grain exports.
    The CORRECT answer is:

    A. I only
    B. II, IV
    C. III only
    D. I, III

7. Which of the following did Roosevelt and Churchill directly cede to Stalin at the 1945 Yalta summit?

    A. Control over the reconstruction of western Berlin
    B. The annexation of Romania
    C. The establishment of socialist governments in the Baltic states
    D. The annexation of parts of eastern Poland

8. The main cause of the great Russian famine of 1921 was

    A. a persistent and widespread drought
    B. the destruction and inaccessibility of lands on the eastern front during World War I
    C. the Bolshevik government's policy regarding agricultural exports
    D. the Bolshevik government's policy for requisitioning grain surpluses

9. Which of the following sectors benefited from Stalin's fourth Five-Year Plan (1946-1951)?

    A. Heavy industry
    B. Agriculture
    C. Housing
    D. Consumer goods

10. In the October Revolution of 1917, who planned and executed the actual coup that toppled the government?

    A. Martov
    B. Trotsky
    C. Stalin
    D. Lenin

11. For what reason did the Japanese bring their attack on Mongolia to a sudden halt in 1939?

    A. Germany and the Soviet Union had just signed a non-aggression pact.
    B. It was clear that the offensive would fail.
    C. Soviet and Japanese diplomats had just agreed to the terms of a nonaggression pact.
    D. Hitler had just invaded Poland.

12. Which of the following was NOT an independent republic after the Bolsheviks defeated the White armies during the civil war of 1918-1920?

    A. Lithuania
    B. The Ukraine
    C. Finland
    D. Latvia

13. In the period immediately following Krushchev's demise, Brezhnev and the oligarchs focused most of their efforts on

    A. stimulating the faltering economy
    B. establishing stability and order
    C. patching up relations with China
    D. decentralizing the decision-making apparatus

14. In the summer of 1942, Hitler ordered an attack on the Soviet Union that was designed to capture the

    A. Baltic states
    B. political and cultural regions in Moscow and Leningrad
    C. *breadbasket* of the Ukraine
    D. industrial regions to the south and eventually the Caucasus

15. Speaking before the Council of Europe in 1989, Mikhail Gorbachev announced that the Soviet Union would

    A. hold the first democratic elections in its history
    B. not interfere in the reform movements of Eastern European countries
    C. cease to aim its nuclear missiles at targets in Western Europe and the United States
    D. withdraw its troops from the former East Germany

16. In Russian history, the *Time of Troubles* refers to the period between the

    A. ascension of Ivan the Terrible and his death
    B. death of Boris Godunov and the accession of Mikhail, the first Romanov tsar
    C. death of Catherine the Great and the accession of Nicholas I
    D. fall of Nicholas II and the implementation of the New Economic Policy

17. The 28th Congress of the Communist Party of the Soviet Union (CPSU), held in July 1990, was a turning point in the struggle for power between

    A. reformers and conservatives
    B. Gorbachev and Yeltsin
    C. the Supreme Soviet and the Congress of People's Deputies (CPD)
    D. moderates and reformers

18. After the Cheka was dissolved in 1922, its functions were absorbed by the organization known as the

    A. MGB   B. NKVD   C. GPU   D. Politburo

19. Under Gorbachev's early definition of *glasnost,* the concept applied mainly to

    A. relaxing censorship in the search for truth
    B. stimulating civic participation in Soviet society
    C. establishing multi-candidate elections for Party posts
    D. exposing waste and abuse in the state bureaucracy

20. Which of the following was NOT an element of the 1971 Four Powers Agreement concerning the administration of Berlin?

    A. All parties pledged not to attempt to change the status of the city.
    B. West Berlin was recognized as part of West Germany.
    C. The Soviets pledged to refrain from communication and transportation into West Berlin.
    D. West Berliners would be allowed to travel with West German passports and receive West German consular protection abroad.

21. In Lenin's *April Theses* of 1917, what did he urge the Bolsheviks to do?
    I. Transfer power to the Soviets
    II. Eliminate the tsar and his family
    III. Support the war effort
    IV. Support the Provisional Government
    The CORRECT answer is:

    A. I only   B. I, IV   C. II, III   D. III, IV

22. Gorbachev's shift to the right in 1991 was illustrated by the central Soviet governments military crackdown on unrest in

    A. Armenia
    B. the Baltics
    C. Chechnya
    D. Georgia

23. The first Five-Year Plan, begun in the late 1920s, was undertaken in part because Soviet leaders believed industry had received inadequate attention and resources under Lenin. Another reason for the implementation of the plan was

    A. a desire to develop an infrastructure adequate for maintaining a hold on power to the east
    B. the desire to mount a show of strength that would deter Hitler's designs on Soviet territory
    C. to create employment for peasants displaced by collectivization
    D. the fear that private enterprise was gaining a foothold in Soviet society

24. Which of the following was NOT a principle of the economic plan unveiled by the Central Committee in June of 1987?

    A. The self-financing of commercial enterprise
    B. Decentralization of economic decision-making
    C. The legalized privatization of large enterprises such as steel
    D. Greater Soviet involvement in the international economy

25. During the reign of Alexander III, the expansion of Russian industrialism was fueled primarily by

    A. foreign investment
    B. tax revenues
    C. grain exports
    D. government subsidy

26. In 1953, the Soviet political police reorganized from the MGB (Ministry of State Security) into the

    A. NKVD (People's Commissariat of Internal Affairs)
    B. MVD (Ministry of Internal Affairs)
    C. NKGB (People's Commissariat of State Security)
    D. KGB (Committee of State Security)

27. Nominally, Stalin's 1936 constitution guaranteed civil rights – including the right to work, rest, vote, and receive medical care and education – for all

    A. Soviet citizens, regardless of gender, ethnicity, or religion
    B. Soviet citizens except women and the clergy
    C. Soviet citizens except the clergy and minority groups
    D. members of the Communist Party

28. The foreign policy legacy that Krushchev left to his successors in the Soviet government could best be described as

    A. an increasingly threatening posture toward Western capitalist economies
    B. slowly improving relations with the United States and increasingly bitter exchanges with the People's Republic of China

C. an overextension of the principle of expansion, which required a retrenchment
D. a general acquiescence to the West on the conditions attached to trade agreements, which needed to be made more firm

29. During the civil war that began in 1918 in Russia, troops from several nations were garrisoned on Russian territory. Which of the following countries did NOT station troops on Russian soil during this time?

    A. Japan
    B. Ottoman Empire
    C. Great Britain
    D. Italy

30. The organization formed in 1918 for indoctrinating Soviet youth in communism was

    A. Sovkhoz
    B. Komsomol
    C. Cominform
    D. Sovnarkam

31. The primary purpose of the *show trials* undertaken by Stalin during the 1930s was to

    A. create a cheap source of labor for the Five-Year Plans
    B. discourage dissent on the part of the masses
    C. delegitimize the church and clerics
    D. eliminate Stalin's political enemies

32. The primary goal of the Soviets' investment in the Vietnam conflict was to

    A. establish a strong, united socialist government from which Soviet interests could be pursued in Southeast Asia
    B. use the situation to worsen relations between the United States and the People's Republic of China
    C. establish a peaceful coexistence in Southeast Asia
    D. deliver a humiliating military defeat to the United States

33. Which of the following was NOT an immediate effect of the emancipation of Russia's serfs by Tsar Alexander II?
    The peasants

    A. were organized into communes
    B. began to have annual redemption dues to compensate the nobles
    C. were assigned family plots that would remain in their custody for the natural life of the eldest male
    D. acquired about two-thirds of the land they had worked

34. Following the sham discovery of the *Doctors' Plot* in 1952-1953, the Soviet government broke off diplomatic relations with

    A. Israel
    B. China
    C. Great Britain
    D. the United States

35. The first serious Soviet-Japanese clash that occurred in the latter part of the 1930s occurred at

    A. Lake Khasan, south of Vladivostok
    B. the Khalkha River in Mongolia
    C. Changkufeng hill, south of Vladivostok
    D. the Manchurian border

36. In the early years of *perestroika,* public support for the process focused on

    A. exposing the injuries of the previous system
    B. relaxing social constraints
    C. democratizing Soviet elections
    D. developing a strong open market

37. The Provisional Government established after the March Revolution of 1917 proved to be relatively weak, for several reasons. The most important factor contributing to this weakness was

    A. the necessity of sharing power with the Soviets
    B. the unlikeliness of fulfilling all of the people's post-revolutionary desires
    C. the lack of a common objective after the monarchy had fallen
    D. being widely regarded as a temporary arrangement

38. Which of the following was the last Soviet city or territory to be liberated from German control during World War II?

    A. Novgorod   B. The Caucasus
    C. The Ukraine   D. Odessa

39. The results of the Bolsheviks' policy of War Communism, adopted in 1918, include
    I. a violent struggle between the new regime and the peasants
    II. strikes by urban workers
    III. an armed revolt against the new regime by aristocrats defending their land
    IV. a general appeasement of the monarchists

    The CORRECT answer is:

    A. I, II   B. II, IV   C. III *only*   D. III, IV

40. In 1939, the League of Nations formally condemned the Soviet Union for its aggression against

    A. Romania   B. Estonia   C. Finland   D. Poland

KEY (CORRECT ANSWERS)

1.	B	11.	A	21.	A	31.	D
2.	C	12.	B	22.	B	32.	B
3.	A	13.	B	23.	D	33.	C
4.	D	14.	D	24.	C	34.	A
5.	B	15.	B	25.	A	35.	A
6.	C	16.	B	26.	B	36.	A
7.	D	17.	B	27.	A	37.	A
8.	D	18.	C	28.	B	38.	C
9.	A	19.	D	29.	B	39.	A
10.	B	20.	B	30.	B	40.	C

TEST 4

DIRECTIONS: Each question or incomplete statement is followed by several suggested answers or completions. Select the one that BEST answers the question or completes the statement. *PRINT THE LETTER OF THE CORRECT ANSWER IN THE SPACE AT THE RIGHT.*

1. In 1949, the Soviet government proudly revealed that more than 100,000 women on collective farms were team leaders and managers. The cause of women's ascendancy in this sector was

    A. fewer educational opportunities for women than for men
    B. a program of reforms that trained and placed women in leadership positions
    C. a surplus of unmarried women who had no household to maintain
    D. the loss of men in World War II

    1._____

2. By the early nineteenth century, the institution of serfdom embraced about _____ % of the Russian population.

    A. 20   B. 40   C. 60   D. 80

    2._____

3. The substance of the secret 1957 agreement between China and the Soviet Union was that the

    A. Soviets would provide nuclear protection in the case of an attack on China
    B. Soviets would back an invasion of Taiwan
    C. Chinese would provide troops in the case of an attack on the Soviet Union
    D. Soviets would supply China with nuclear technology.

    3._____

4. The treaty of Brest-Litovsk, signed by Russia in 1918 to effect its extrication from World War I, temporarily deprived Russia of control over each of the following EXCEPT

    A. Finland   B. the Transcaucasus
    C. the Ukraine   D. the Baltic states

    4._____

5. from 1956 to 1958, the Soviet government withdrew Stalin's former charges of treason and collaboration from the ethnic minorities who had been deported, and most were allowed to return to their homelands. Which of the following groups was NOT allowed to repatriate?

    A. Karachai   B. Crimean Tatars
    C. Chechen   D. Kalmyks

    5._____

6. After the February Revolution of 1917, it was widely taken for granted among Russian revolutionaries that the new state would become a(n)

    A. autocracy
    B. republic
    C. proletarian dictatorship
    D. constitutional monarchy

    6._____

7. During the Brezhnev era, the Soviet people became increasingly dissatisfied with economic conditions, and yet society remained remarkably calm. Each of the following was a reason for this EXCEPT

    7._____

101

A. aggressive punishments of dissenters by the KGB
B. total Communist party control of institutions
C. the relative availability of most consumer goods
D. the complacency of Soviet citizens in the face of relative stability

8. Which of the following nations withdrew from the Warsaw Pact in 1968?

    A. Romania
    B. Hungary
    C. Albania
    D. Czechoslovakia

9. Which of the following was NOT an element of Yuri Andropov's economic program?

    A. Reducing government corruption
    B. The linkage of managers' salaries to profits
    C. Tighter control of manufacturing and agricultural enterprises
    D. Providing incentives for productive workers

10. A clear result of the *Kornilov Affair* of 1917 was a

    A. revival of the use of martial law among Russian leaders
    B. persistent counterrevolutionary attitude among a minority of Russians
    C. widespread desire for a stronger military
    D. weakening of the Provisional Government

11. The marriage decree of 1944, which nullified all common- law marriages and made divorce more difficult, was designed by the Stalin government to do each of the following EXCEPT

    A. create the appearance of adherence to church doctrines
    B. spur population growth
    C. provide a future labor force
    D. replace wartime losses

12. Mikhail Bakunin, a 19th-century intellectual reformist, called for

    A. the adaptation of socialism to Russian conditions, to foment a peasant revolution
    B. a return to the Russian state as it existed before the introduction of Western ideas
    C. the creation of a society that would abolish the Russian Church and in which no class was dominant
    D. the assassination of the governor of St. Petersburg

13. Which of the following was NOT a reason for the strong resistance to the German invasions of western Soviet territories in World War II?
    The

    A. devotion to the socialist cause and the Soviet government
    B. Germans' inhumane treatment of prisoners of war
    C. exploitation of the peasantry by the German invaders
    D. Germans' failure to address the political hopes of Soviet minorities

14. Which of the following nations signed the international Non-Proliferation Treaty of 1968?
    I. The Soviet Union
    II. France
    III. The United States
    IV. Spain
    V. India
    The CORRECT answer is:

    A. I, III	B. I, II, III, IV	C. II, III, V	D. I, II, V

15. In the late 1940s, which of the following tended to function most INEFFICIENTLY in the Soviet Union?

    A. Steel mills	B. The secret police
    C. Retail stores	D. The Moscow subway

16. The *Alpha Team* was

    A. the segment of the secret police in the days of the OGPU which arrested citizens for thought crimes
    B. the group of hard-line communists who attempted to overthrow the Gorbachev government in 1991
    C. the group responsible for cultural reforms under Lenin's post-revolutionary government
    D. a Soviet counter-terrorism unit that attacked civilians in Vilnius in 1991

17. Although Russia was the more powerful nation, it lost the Russo-Japanese War of 1904-1905. Which of the following was NOT a significant factor contributing to this loss?

    A. British support of the Japanese
    B. Greater popular support in Japan for the war effort
    C. Inadequate Russian infrastructure for material delivery eastward
    D. Japanese naval superiority

18. Which of the following was a result of the Cuban missile crisis?

    A. The erosion of Krushchev's support within the Communist Party
    B. An economic crisis in Cuba
    C. A loss of respect for Krushchev among Western leaders
    D. An improvement in Sino-Soviet relations

19. During the Brezhnev years, each of the following was typically among the top echelon of party leaders EXCEPT

    A. Konstantin Chernenko	B. Mikhail Gorbachev
    C. Andrei Kirilenko	D. Mikhail Suslov

20. Which of the following countries invaded disputed Russian territory in 1920?

    A. Sweden	B. Japan	C. China	D. Poland

21. Which of the following political groups did NOT support the succession of Yuri Andropov as successor to Brezhnev?

    A. The military	B. Old-line Communists
    C. The KGB	D. Party technocrats

22. For what reason did Stalin fire commissar of foreign affairs Maxim Litvinov in 1939? 22.____
    A. Litvinov had botched the attempt to patch things up with Japan.
    B. He had publicly denounced Stalin's intention to sign a nonaggression pact with Hitler.
    C. He was a Jew and an obstacle to any pact with Hitler.
    D. He disapproved of the secret protocol of the non-aggression pact with Hitler.

23. In 1988, Gorbachev announced the complete separation of the CPSU from the area of _____ decision-making. 23.____
    A. military   B. social   C. judicial   D. economic

24. For what reason was Communist International, or Comintern, abolished in 1943? 24.____
    A. Its primary goal of sovietizing Germany was set aside for the war effort.
    B. Stalin was no longer an adherent to the ideals of Bolshevism.
    C. It was a gesture of goodwill toward the Western Allies,
    D. It would soon be rendered superfluous by the Soviet occupation of Eastern Europe.

25. The ideals of the Slavophiles, a revolutionary group that arose in the nineteenth century, included each of the following EXCEPT 25.____
    A. an autocracy free of bureaucratic interference
    B. a purified Orthodox church
    C. increased reliance on Western technology
    D. a reliance on the peasant commune

26. The clearest result of the *changing landmarks* movement of the 1920s was a 26.____
    A. firmly established counterrevolutionary movement
    B. move toward an even more centralized government
    C. new legitimacy for the Bolsheviks
    D. sense of history being temporarily disrupted by revolution

27. For what reason was St. Petersburg renamed Petrograd during World War I? 27.____
    A. Russian leaders thought *St. Petersburg* was too Germanic in origin.
    B. The capital had been moved to Moscow.
    C. Lenin wanted to prepare the people for its eventual name, Leningrad.
    D. Leaders wanted to eliminate any implication of religiosity from the name.

28. In what year was the *Curzon Line* established, marking the border between Poland and Soviet Russia? 28.____
    A. 1918   B. 1921   C. 1939   D. 1945

29. Judging from the conduct of the *show trials* of the 1930s, the most important lesson Stalin seemed to have learned from the Shakhty trial of 1928 was that 29.____
    A. the public was not fooled by attempts at scapegoating
    B. too many defendants detracted from the public impact of a trial
    C. the legal system could be manipulated to suit the will of the party
    D. the only trials in which the people took an interest were ones involving direct violations against the working class

30. The aftermath of the Russo-Japanese War (1904-1905) included each of the following conditions in Russia EXCEPT

    A. mounting popular demands for a legislative assembly
    B. an increase in taxation
    C. a surge of nationalist sentiment
    D. a weakening of the prestige of the tsar's government

31. Which of the following were factors that led to the stagnation of the Soviet economy in the 1970s?
    I. Low birth rates in European Russia
    II. Bad weather
    III. Failure of the 1972 United States trade pact
    IV. Alcoholism

    The CORRECT answer is:

    A. I, II
    B. II *only*
    C. I, II, IV
    D. III, IV

32. Lenin's *April Theses,* while shocking to outsiders, were also a shock to many Bolsheviks, because he

    A. proposed a death sentence for the tsar
    B. called upon the Bolsheviks to build up majorities in the Soviets and then work to transfer power to them
    C. demanded tribute in the form of food and grains from the peasant farmers
    D. advocated the immediate transition to socialism after overthrowing the monarchy, instead of going through an intermediate capitalist phase

33. For what reason had the number of Soviet livestock fallen in 1934 to less than half of the 1928 figure?

    A. Animals were being exported to finance the Five-Year Plan.
    B. Peasants were killing off animals to protest collectivization.
    C. Environmental pollution was interfering with animal reproduction.
    D. Widespread famine had made food too scarce for animals.

34. The 1980 political crisis in Poland was precipitated by

    A. government censorship of mainstream media
    B. a government crackdown on illegal labor strikes
    C. a reduction in workers' pensions
    D. the government's withdrawal of price supports from meat

35. Which director of the secret police presided over the bloodiest era of the Stalin purges?

    A. Yezhov
    B. Menzhinsky
    C. Beria
    D. Dzerzhinsky

36. After the Moscow government freed price controls on several luxury items in 1990, three republics declared U.S.S.R. law nonbinding on their citizens. Which of the following was NOT one of these republics?

    A. Russia
    B. Ukraine
    C. Azerbaijan
    D. Kazakhstan

37. During the ear of the NEP, the Soviet government pursued a foreign policy that has been described as *bi-level* in nature. The best illustration of this policy is

    A. making concessions on an economic level, while sticking to strictly favorable terms on the political level
    B. alienating the upper classes while luring the support of the working and farming classes
    C. cooperation and normalization on an official level, while Comintern worked secretly to foment communist revolution
    D. an isolationist policy regarding foreign assistance and an expansionist policy

38. During the Russian civil war of 1918-1920, which of the following countries sent soldiers to occupy Russian territory and aid the White armies?

    A. Japan
    B. Poland
    C. France
    D. The United States

39. The *troika* that ruled the Communist Party from 1964-1971 included each of the following EXCEPT

    A. Leonid Brezhnev
    B. Anastas Mikoyan
    C. Alexei Kosygin
    D. Mikhail Suslov

40. The SALT I agreement of 1972, between the United States and the Soviet Union, included limitations on the
    I. number of missile-carrying planes that could be constructed
    II. number of each nation's offensive nuclear weapons
    III. number of missile-carrying submarines that could be constructed
    IV. deployment of anti-ballistic missiles

    The CORRECT answer is:

    A. I, III
    B. II, IV
    C. II, III, IV
    D. I, IV

KEY (CORRECT ANSWERS)

1. D	11. A	21. B	31. C
2. D	12. C	22. C	32. D
3. D	13. A	23. D	33. B
4. B	14. A	24. C	34. D
5. B	15. C	25. C	35. A
6. B	16. D	26. C	36. B
7. C	17. C	27. A	37. C
8. C	18. A	28. B	38. A
9. C	19. B	29. B	39. B
10. D	20. D	30. C	40. C

EXAMINATION SECTION
TEST 1

DIRECTIONS: Each question or incomplete statement is followed by several suggested answers or completions. Select the one that BEST answers the question or completes the statement. *PRINT THE LETTER OF THE CORRECT ANSWER IN THE SPACE AT THE RIGHT.*

1. Institutional opposition to *glasnost* and democratization in the Soviet Union involved which of the following?
    I. Communist party of the Soviet Union
    II. State security police (KGB)
    III. Military
    IV. Bureaucracy
   The CORRECT answer is:

   A. I *only*
   B. II, IV
   C. I, II, III
   D. I, III, IV
   E. I, II, III, IV

2. A PRINCIPAL difference between reform in China and in the Soviet Union between 1980 and 1990 was that

   A. economic reform was more successful in China than in the Soviet Union
   B. the Chinese Communist party was more open to multiparty competition than was the Soviet party
   C. nationalist movements were more important in China than in the Soviet Union
   D. Soviet reformers were more successful in establishing deep and comprehensive commercial relations with Western industrialized countries than were Chinese reformers
   E. Soviet reformers were more hostile to Western philosophies and practices than were Chinese reformers

3. In the Soviet Union between 1953 and 1985, the center of policy-making power was the

   A. Supreme Soviet
   B. Red Army
   C. state security police (KGB)
   D. Politburo
   E. Council of Ministers

4. Which of the following contributed MOST to the instability of the Soviet Union in the late 1980's?

   A. Persistent ethnic and national demands for self-determination
   B. Increase in the power of the Communist party
   C. Economic integration among constituent republics
   D. Support for nationalist movements by foreign powers
   E. Unwillingness of the government of the Russian Republic to play a leadership role

5. MAJOR accomplishments under Gorbachev's leadership in the Soviet Union from 1985 to 1991 included which of the following?
   I. Negotiating treaties to reduce nuclear arms
   II. Rebuilding Soviet transportation systems to bring agricultural produce to the cities
   III. Converting the ruble to the gold standard
   IV. Reducing restrictions on freedom of speech and the press

   The CORRECT answer is:

   A. II only
   B. I, III
   C. I, IV
   D. II, III
   E. I, III, IV

6. The political system of the Soviet Union between 1965 and 1985 was characterized by

   A. a government apparatus that dominated the Communist party
   B. a highly stable political elite
   C. a politically dominant military
   D. domination of the legislature by non-Slavic groups
   E. regional governments that tended to dominate the national government

7. Of the following, the Soviet regime was generally MOST successful at

   A. educating its citizens
   B. expanding agricultural production for national self-sufficiency
   C. developing and using technology to meet consumer demands
   D. earning hard currency through the export of high technology
   E. maintaining balanced economic growth

8. In the Soviet Union, the term *nomenklatura* referred to the

   A. pattern of repeated Western military interventions into Third World politics
   B. system by which party leaders could be removed from office
   C. system of patron-client relations that the Soviet Union promoted with developing countries
   D. system by which the Communist party controlled key positions in government and industry
   E. links between the Communist party of the Soviet Union and Third World Communist parties

9. All of the following are correct statements about the reform process in the former Soviet Union EXCEPT:

   A. Gorbachev was elected President of the Soviet Union by direct popular election
   B. Forces opposed to the reform process attempted to seize power through a *coup d'état,* but were unsuccessful
   C. Difficulties resulting from the reform process weakened the power of the central government and strengthened the power of the governments of the republics
   D. Reforms allowed organized religion to play a more important role in society
   E. The reform process greatly weakened the power of the Communist party

10. During the mid-1980's, the Soviet Union experimented with modifications of its command economy by

A. eliminating central planning
B. allowing private ownership of major industries
C. introducing some market economy strategies
D. legalizing independent trade unions

Question 11.

DIRECTIONS: Question 11 is to be answered on the basis of the quotation below and on your knowledge of social studies.

From Stettin in the Baltic to Trieste in the Adriatic, an iron curtain has descended across the Continent. Behind that line lie all the capitals of the ancient states of central and eastern Europe. Warsaw, Berlin, Prague, Vienna, Budapest, Belgrade, Bucharest, and Sofia, all these famous cities and the populations around them lie in what I might call the Soviet sphere, and all are subject, in one form or another, not only to Soviet influence, but to very high, and in some cases increasing measure of control from Moscow.

11. What is the MAIN idea of this quotation? The

    A. Soviet Union has expanded its influence throughout eastern Europe
    B. Soviet Union has helped the nations of eastern Europe improve their standard of living
    C. democratic nations of western Europe have stopped the expansion of Soviet influence in the world
    D. Soviet Union will support communist revolutions in Southeast Asia

12. Which statement BEST describes the political situation in the Soviet Union immediately after Lenin's death in 1924?

    A. The nation adopted a constitutional monarchy.
    B. Trotsky and his followers assumed full control of the Communist Party.
    C. Popular elections were held to choose a new General Secretary.
    D. A power struggle developed among Communist Party leaders.

13. The Russian peasants supported the Bolsheviks in the 1917 revolutions MAINLY because the Bolsheviks promised to

    A. establish collective farms
    B. maintain the agricultural price-support system
    C. bring modern technology to Russian farms
    D. redistribute the land owned by the nobility

14. Which term BEST describes the political system in Russia before the 20th century?

    A. Constitutional republic   B. Absolute monarchy
    C. Parliamentary democracy   D. Military dictatorship

15. Which has been a MAJOR change in the political situation in Western Europe in the last half of the 20th century?

    A. Nationalism has increased rivalry between Western European nations.

B. Western European nations have gained power through control of world oil resources.
C. Western European nations have worked cooperatively for security and prosperity.
D. Powerful dictatorships have emerged throughout Western Europe.

16. Which statement BEST describes Europe just before World War I?

    A. The formation of opposing alliance systems increased international distrust.
    B. European leaders resorted to a policy of appeasement to solve international disputes.
    C. The communist nations promoted violent revolution throughout Western Europe.
    D. The isolationist policies of England and France prevented their entry into the hostilities.

17. Karl Marx believed that a proletarian revolution was MORE likely to occur as a society became more

    A. religious
    B. militarized
    C. industrialized
    D. democratic

18. During the 1980's in the Soviet Union, a MAJOR element of the economic policy of *perestroika* was

    A. increased collectivization of farms
    B. more reliance on local and regional decision-making
    C. the expanded use of national five-year plans
    D. an emphasis on the redistribution of wealth

19. The events that took place in Hungary in the 1950's and in Czechoslovakia in the 1960's demonstrated the Soviet Union's

    A. support of nationalism among satellite nations
    B. influence on the economies of developing nations
    C. determination to maintain political control over Eastern Europe at that time
    D. attempts to promote its artistic and literary achievements in Western Europe

20. The political reorganization of Russia after the Communist Revolution of 1917 resulted in

    A. the establishment of a two-party political system
    B. increased political power for ethnic minorities
    C. a limited monarchy with the Czar as a figurehead
    D. a federation of socialist republics

21. A problem that faced the Austro-Hungarian Empire, the Ottoman Empire, and the Soviet Union is the

    A. effect of urbanization on a rural population
    B. monopoly of the traditional church
    C. inability to produce modern weapons
    D. tension between many different ethnic groups

22. A study of the causes of the American, French, and Russian Revolutions indicates that revolutions USUALLY occur because the

   A. society has become dependent on commerce and trade
   B. society has a lower standard of living than the societies around it
   C. existing government has been resistant to change
   D. lower classes have strong leaders

23. The economy of the Soviet Union differed MOST from the economy of the United States in the

   A. emphasis placed on technological development
   B. need for skilled workers
   C. manner of deciding which goods were produced
   D. importance given to production of military weapons

24. The MAIN purpose of the many purges and public trials that took place in the Soviet Union in the 1930's was to

   A. force the Jewish people to leave the Soviet Union
   B. eliminate opposition to Joseph Stalin and his government
   C. establish a free and independent court system in the Soviet Union
   D. reform the outdated and inadequate agricultural system

25. A MAJOR reason many Russian people supported the Bolsheviks in the November 1917 revolution was that the Bolsheviks called for

   A. an immediate peace settlement with Germany
   B. a heavy investment in industry
   C. the collectivization of agriculture
   D. the abolition of all religion

KEY (CORRECT ANSWERS)

1.	E	11.	A
2.	A	12.	D
3.	D	13.	D
4.	A	14.	B
5.	C	15.	C
6.	B	16.	A
7.	A	17.	C
8.	D	18.	B
9.	A	19.	C
10.	C	20.	D

21. D
22. C
23. C
24. B
25. A

TEST 2

DIRECTIONS: Each question or incomplete statement is followed by several suggested answers or completions. Select the one that BEST answers the question or completes the statement. *PRINT THE LETTER OF THE CORRECT ANSWER IN THE SPACE AT THE RIGHT.*

1. The history of Russia was influenced by its lack of

    A. warm-water ports
    B. mineral deposits
    C. different climates
    D. navigable river systems

    1.___

2. Communist philosophy teaches that people should

    A. revere their ancestors and religious traditions
    B. obey their rulers because they have authority from heaven
    C. reject technology and Western values
    D. place the interests of the group before the interests of the individual

    2.___

3. Which statement BEST reflects the theories of Karl Marx and Friedrich Engels?

    A. Workers can expect that working conditions will improve as a result of government legislation.
    B. Owners of businesses will eventually realize that conditions for workers must be improved.
    C. Workers will experience an improved standard of living as capitalism matures.
    D. Workers will change working conditions by revolutionary means.

    3.___

4. A study of Yugoslavia, the People's Republic of China, and the Soviet Union during the 1980's would BEST indicate that Marxism

    A. achieved its goal of a classless society
    B. was formally discontinued by all three countries
    C. is often reshaped to meet the particular needs of the government
    D. is practiced strictly in accordance with Karl Marx's ideas

    4.___

5. Joseph Stalin's leadership of the Soviet Union can BEST be characterized as a period of

    A. democratic reform and nationalism
    B. humanism and democracy
    C. religious freedom and tolerance
    D. censorship and terror

    5.___

6. Which is GENERALLY a characteristic of a communist economy?

    A. Investment is encouraged by the promise of large profits
    B. The role of government in the economy is restricted by law
    C. Government agencies are involved in production planning
    D. Entrepreneurs sell shares in their companies to the government

    6.___

7. In the 1980's, the MAJOR ostensible source of the conflict between Israel and Palestinian Arabs was

    A. the presence of Israeli ships in the Suez Canal
    B. the interference of Libya in Middle Eastern affairs
    C. the demand of Palestinian Arabs for their own homeland
    D. Soviet support of radical Arab groups in occupied territories

    7.___

8. In the 1970's, when Iran was ruled by the Shah, the Ayatollah Khomeini's MAJOR criticism was of the

   A. Shah's friendship with the Soviet Union
   B. return to traditional Islamic law
   C. lack of political and social rights for women
   D. non-Islamic influences on the culture and economy

9. Which generalization is BEST supported by developments in trade such as Japanese investments in Southeast Asia, the sale of United States grain to the Soviet Union, and the reliance of many Western European nations on oil from the Middle East?

   A. Most of the nations of the world are adopting socialist economies.
   B. Nations that control vital resources are no longer able to influence world markets.
   C. The goal of the world's economic planners is to decrease national self-sufficiency.
   D. The nations of the world have become interdependent.

10. The withdrawal of France from Indochina, the involvement of the Soviet Union in Cuba, and the United States support of the Contras in Nicaragua illustrated that nations

    A. consistently discard traditional foreign policy goals after changes in administration
    B. tend to base foreign policy decisions on what they believe to be their self-interests
    C. no longer use warfare as a means to resolve international conflict
    D. tend to refer foreign policy conflicts to the United Nations

11. A study of revolutions would MOST likely lead to the conclusion that pre-revolutionary governments

    A. are more concerned about human rights than the governments that replace them are
    B. refuse to modernize their armed forces with advanced technology
    C. attempt to bring about the separation of government from religion
    D. fail to meet the political and economic needs of their people

12. The North Atlantic Treaty Organization, the Cuban Missile Crisis, and the Korean War are examples of

    A. attempts to prevent the spread of communist power
    B. United States efforts to gain foreign territory
    C. the failure of capitalism and free market economies
    D. United Nations interference in the internal affairs of member nations

13. During the 1980's, a nation that was nonaligned and economically developing would MOST likely have

    A. entered into an exclusive trade agreement with the United States
    B. joined the other members of the Warsaw Pact
    C. formed a military alliance with the Soviet Union
    D. accepted aid from both the Soviet Union and the United States

14. Which statement BEST described the political situation in Eastern Europe during the 1980's?

    A. Nationalism was a strong force for change.
    B. Communist governments gained power through democratic elections.
    C. Ethnic rivalries were eliminated throughout the region.
    D. United States influence was used to keep communist governments in power.

15. The Soviet Union's reaction to the 1968 revolt in Czechoslovakia was to

    A. permit limited political and economic reforms in Czechoslovakia
    B. withdraw Soviet troops from Eastern Europe
    C. send Soviet troops to occupy Czechoslovakia
    D. bring the matter to the attention of the United Nations

16. The economic policies of the Soviet Union traditionally emphasized the production of

    A. automobiles for export
    B. building materials for luxury housing
    C. consumer goods
    D. heavy industrial goods

17. Which statement BEST describes most Eastern European countries immediately after World War II?
    They

    A. adopted democratic reforms in their political systems
    B. became satellite states of the Soviet Union
    C. became dependent on aid provided by the Marshall Plan
    D. emerged as world economic powers

18. A MAJOR cause of the Russian Revolution of 1917 was the

    A. defeat of Germany in the Russian campaign
    B. marriage of Czar Nicholas II to a German princess
    C. existence of sharp economic differences between social classes
    D. appeal of Marxism to the Russian nobility

19. Which was a characteristic of Germany under Adolf Hitler and the Soviet Union under Josef Stalin?

    A. An official foreign policy of isolationism
    B. Governmental control of the media
    C. Public ownership of business and industry
    D. The absence of a written constitution

20. Which statement BEST describes the relationship between World War I and the Russian Revolution?

    A. World War I created conditions within Russia that helped trigger a revolution.
    B. World War I postponed the Russian Revolution by restoring confidence in the Czar.
    C. The Russian Revolution inspired the Russian people to win World War I.
    D. World War I gave the Czar's army the needed experience to suppress the Russian Revolution.

Question 21.

DIRECTIONS: Question 21 is to be answered on the basis of the passage below and on your knowledge of social studies.

ARTICLE 50. In accordance with the interests of the people and in order to strengthen and develop the socialist system, citizens of the USSR are guaranteed freedom of speech, of the press, and of assembly, meetings, street processions, and demonstrations.

Exercise of these political freedoms is ensured by putting public buildings, streets, and squares at the disposal of the working people and their organizations, by broad dissemination of information, and by the opportunity to use the press, television, and radio.

21. Which conclusion can be reached by a comparison of events in the Soviet Union and the above passage from the Constitution of the Soviet Union?

    A. Constitutional rights guarantee a free society.
    B. A national constitution always guarantees human rights.
    C. A constitutional guarantee must be very specific in order to be effective.
    D. A constitutional guarantee may be limited by government actions.

Question 22.

DIRECTIONS: Question 22 is to be answered on the basis of the cartoon shown on the following page and on your knowledge of social studies.

22. What is the MAIN idea of the cartoon? Communism

    A. is open to all classes of society
    B. has become increasingly more powerful
    C. has lost sight of its original goals
    D. is no longer taken seriously

23. Westernization of Russia came about LARGELY through the

    A. efforts of Peter the Great and his successors
    B. invasion of Russia by Sweden
    C. desire of the United States to seek new markets
    D. acceptance of the policies of the Eastern Orthodox Church

24. According to Karl Marx, which is the MAJOR determining factor in history?

    A. Conflict among religions
    B. Effectiveness of political leadership
    C. Competition for control of territory
    D. Struggle among economic classes

25. A BASIC economic difference between capitalism and socialism concerns the issue of the

    A. role of the government in controlling public education
    B. role of trade in achieving national prosperity
    C. ownership of the means of production and distribution
    D. amount of resources spent on industrial expansion

KEY (CORRECT ANSWERS)

1. A
2. D
3. D
4. C
5. D

6. C
7. C
8. D
9. D
10. B

11. D
12. A
13. D
14. A
15. C

16. D
17. B
18. C
19. B
20. A

21. D
22. C
23. A
24. D
25. C

TEST 3

DIRECTIONS: Each question or incomplete statement is followed by several suggested answers or completions. Select the one that BEST answers the question or completes the statement. *PRINT THE LETTER OF THE CORRECT ANSWER IN THE SPACE AT THE RIGHT.*

1. During the decade following World War II, the _____ was a MAJOR cause of tension in Europe.

    A. formation of Soviet-dominated Communist governments in many Eastern European nations
    B. failure of the non-Communist countries to support the United Nations
    C. cutbacks in fuel supplies by oil-producing nations
    D. return of United States military forces to pre-World War II levels

    1.____

2. In which area did the views of the United States and the Soviet Union differ MOST before glasnost?

    A. Belief in the importance of a strong national defense
    B. Desire to influence international events
    C. Interest in the exploration of outer space
    D. Attitudes toward free expression and individual right

    2.____

3. Recognition by both the United States and the Soviet Union of their mutual ability to destroy the world had encouraged both nations at times to

    A. place greater emphasis on the United Nations as a peacemaker
    B. engage in direct combat with each other using conventional weapons
    C. seek ways of controlling the spread of nuclear weapons
    D. place great emphasis on civil defense programs

    3.____

4. Détente, as applied to interaction between the United States and the Soviet Union, was BEST described as a

    A. joint policy to reduce tensions and improve relations
    B. joint policy to improve peace prospects in the Middle East
    C. United States policy of protection for Soviet dissidents
    D. Soviet policy of seeking loans and trade with the United States

    4.____

5. The economy of the Soviet Union differed MOST from the economy of the United States in that, in the Soviet Union,

    A. all workers received the same wages
    B. prices were controlled by the workers
    C. the government determined what was to be produced
    D. working conditions were superior to those in the United States

    5.____

6. A basic difference between communism and capitalism is that, in a communist economic system,

    A. there is a small demand for consumer goods
    B. major industries are under the direction of labor unions

    6.____

C. industry planning is controlled by the government
D. monopolies are illegal

7. After the end of World War II, United States government policy toward the Soviet Union was influenced PRIMARILY by the

   A. existence of Soviet control in Eastern European countries
   B. close alliance between the United States and China
   C. abundance of Soviet aid during the war
   D. cooperation between Soviet and American scientists on nuclear projects

8. A significant cultural aspect of life in many Communist nations had been the

   A. organized social and economic discrimination against women
   B. emphasis upon athletics and other forms of non-economic competition
   C. restraints upon the development of social welfare programs
   D. encouragement of free creative efforts of writers and composers

9. Which quotation about the nature of history BEST describes Karl Marx's basis for communism?

   A. The history of the world is but the biography of great men.
   B. History is made out of the failures and heroism of each significant moment.
   C. The history of all hitherto existing society is the history of class struggles.
   D. Those who cannot remember the past are condemned to repeat it.

10. Which action taken by the government of the Soviet Union had been MOST consistent with Marxist philosophy?

    A. Purchasing wheat from the United States
    B. Giving financial rewards to Soviet athletes
    C. Supplying aid to urban worker revolutionaries in industrialized countries
    D. Adopting a policy of detente toward the United States

11. The event that BEST illustrates the application of the Monroe Doctrine in United States foreign policy is the

    A. establishment of the North Atlantic Treaty Organization (NATO)
    B. Berlin airlift
    C. Cuban missile crisis
    D. declaration of war against Germany in World War II

12. Which one of the following conferences provided for restoration of territory to Russia which she had lost as a result of the Treaty of Portsmouth?

    A. Yalta   B. Potsdam   C. Cairo   D. Teheran

13. During the period immediately preceding the outbreak of World War II, which is the CORRECT chronological order of the following events?
    I. Absorption by Germany of Bohemia and Moravia as a protectorate
    II. Annexation to Germany of Austria
    III. Annexation to Germany of the Sudentenland
    IV. Nazi-Soviet non-aggression pact
    The CORRECT answer is:

    A. II, III, I, IV   B. IV, III, II, I   C. III, II, I, IV   D. I, IV, II, III

14. The CHIEF purpose of the New Economic Policy of the Union of Soviet Socialist Republics was to

    A. bring all the land together into collective farms
    B. bar concessions to foreign investors
    C. restore private ownership in small industries
    D. forbid the private sale of grain by peasants

14._____

15. Which of the following is a TRUE statement about geographic conditions in Russia?

    A. Parts of the Black Sea coast receive almost 100 inches of rainfall annually.
    B. The severity of the climate is moderated by the influence of the bordering oceans.
    C. Summer temperatures along the Arctic coast rarely exceed 32° Fahrenheit.
    D. Over 40% of the country is mountainous and exceeds 6,560 feet in elevation.

15._____

16. On which one of the following issues did Stalin and Trotsky DISAGREE sharply after 1926?

    A. Encouragement of farm collectivization
    B. Possibility of successfully establishing socialism in one country
    C. Inherent weakness of capitalism
    D. Economic planning to control and direct social change

16._____

17. The two Soviet writers arrested in September 1965 and charged with treason for engaging in anti-Soviet propaganda by publishing materials outside the Soviet Union under pseudonyms were

    A. Shokolov and Penkovsky
    B. Menshutin and Pasternack
    C. Mayakovsky and Prokofieff
    D. Sinyavsky and Daniel

17._____

18. In which one of the following pairs dealing with the Cold War was the FIRST item a cause of the SECOND?

    A. Attack on South Korea - Formation of NATO
    B. Guerrilla war in Greece - Truman Doctrine
    C. Hungarian revolt - Geneva Conference of 1954
    D. U-2 Incident - Agency of International Development

18._____

19. Of the following, which one BEST explains the reason why Russia failed to westernize before 1700?

    A. Expansion to the southeast was blocked by the Ural Mountains.
    B. Throughout the 17th century, the church was controlled by the eastern oriented patriarch in Constantinople.
    C. Sweden and Poland prevented open commercial contact through the Baltic.
    D. The Mongols and Tartars exacted heavy tribute on all trade routes.

19._____

20. The French Revolution of 1789 and the Russian Revolution of 1917 were SIMILAR in that

    A. both occurred in conjunction with an unsuccessful war
    B. both were led by professional revolutionaries who had worked for revolution long in advance
    C. both occurred in countries which were economically backward relative to the rest of Europe
    D. in both there was conflict among the revolutionary groups after the immediate overthrow of the *Old Regime*

21. Prior to World War I, the LEADING advocate of industrialization in Russia was

    A. Count Witte
    B. Von Plehve
    C. Alexander Herzen
    D. Constantine Pobiedonostsev

22. The *cordon sanitaire* refers to the

    A. belt of states from Finland to Rumania formed to prevent the westward expansion of Communism after World War I
    B. coalition of Arab states formed to encircle Israel after World War II
    C. boycott organized to weaken the Japanese economy and thus strike at Japanese aggression in China in the 1930's
    D. belt of states formed in eastern Europe to protect the Union of Soviet Socialist Republics against anti-Communist agitation after World War II

23. The Treaty of Rapallo (1922) was SIGNIFICANT because it

    A. reflected the anti-Communist orientation of the German officer corps
    B. marked a relaxation of the isolation of the Soviet Union after World War I
    C. made it more difficult for Germany to evade some of the provisions of the Treaty of Versailles
    D. completed the encirclement of the Soviet Union by hostile powers after World War I

24. Which one of the following formulated the theory on which the government's policy of containment was based?

    A. George F. Kennan
    B. Arthur H. Vandenberg
    C. George C. Marshall
    D. John Foster Fulles

25. Which one of the following events occurred FIRST in time? The

    A. organization of the North Atlantic Treaty Organization
    B. Marshall Plan for European economic recovery
    C. Communist coup in Czechoslovakia
    D. enactment of the Point-Four Program

KEY (CORRECT ANSWERS)

1. A
2. D
3. C
4. A
5. C

6. C
7. A
8. B
9. C
10. C

11. C
12. A
13. A
14. C
15. A

16. B
17. D
18. B
19. C
20. D

21. A
22. A
23. B
24. A
25. B

TEST 4

DIRECTIONS: Each question or incomplete statement is followed by several suggested answers or completions. Select the one that BEST answers the question or completes the statement. *PRINT THE LETTER OF THE CORRECT ANSWER IN THE SPACE AT THE RIGHT.*

1. Following the abdication of the Russian Czar in the spring of 1917, the provisional government of Prince Lvov

    A. restored full autonomy to the Ukraine
    B. ordered the execution of Czar Nicholas II
    C. negotiated the Treaty of Brest-Litovsk with the Central Powers
    D. continued Russia's participation in World War I

2. The Estonian, Latvian, and Lithuanian Republics were

    A. independent before the First World War but were added to the former U.S.S.R. between 1918 and 1939
    B. part of czarist Russia before the First World War and were independent 1918-1939
    C. part of Russia from 1815 to the present time
    D. independent from 1815 until their annexation by the former Soviet Union following the Second World War in 1945

3. Which of the following agreements at Yalta became a MAJOR source of later disagreement between the Allies and the Soviet Union? The

    A. division of East Prussia between the Soviet Union and Poland
    B. future organization of the Polish government
    C. entry of the Soviet Union into the war in the Far East
    D. cession of Far Eastern territories to the Soviet Union

4. The Revolution of 1905 in Russia resembled the French Revolution of 1789 because in both revolutions

    A. a middle class minority sought representative government
    B. socialism played an important role for industrial workers
    C. the interests of peasants were ignored
    D. rulers were able to prevent the establishment of a representative assembly

5. Which one of the following describes Europe in the period 1905-1914? The

    A. middle and upper classes lost their political and cultural leadership
    B. discontent of subject nationalities declined
    C. working class became more militant in an effort to satisfy its grievances
    D. role of the state was reduced with rising living standards

6. Which one of the following was TRUE of the Paris Peace Settlements of World War I?

    A. The wishes and aspirations of Slavic nationalities were ignored.
    B. Russia and Germany were integrated into the new European political structure.
    C. France's demand for a security pact was satisfied.
    D. There was serious neglect of the long-range economic problems of Europe.

7. Andrei D. Sinyavsky and Yuli M. Daniel attracted international attention because they

    A. were the first to walk in space
    B. were imprisoned for anti-Soviet writings
    C. shared the Nobel Prize for physics
    D. were arrested in Peking for espionage

8. According to Karl Marx's view of historical development, which one of the following would bring about the other three?

    A. *Withering away of the state*
    B. *Dictatorship of the proletariat*
    C. *Expropriation of the expropriators*
    D. *A classless society*

9. In emancipating the serfs in 1861, Tsar Alexander II

    A. weakened the Russian aristocracy
    B. made most of the peasants independent landowners
    C. made peasant lands the collective property of the peasant village
    D. allowed peasants full freedom to leave their villages

10. In entering into the Triple Entente with France and Russia in 1907, England agreed to

    A. demarcate British and Russian spheres of influence in Persia
    B. give France a free hand in the Sudan
    C. give Russia control of the Straits
    D. assign France a sphere of influence in Syria

11. Which one of the following occurred FIRST?

    A. Uprising of the Petrograd Soviet
    B. Decembrist Revolt
    C. Bloody Sunday
    D. November Revolution

12. Which of the following authors have written standard works on Russian history?
    I. H. Seton-Watson
    II. P.T. Moon
    III. B. Pares
    IV. E.H. Carr
    V. C.J.H. Hayes

    The CORRECT answer is:

    A. I, II, III
    B. I, III, IV
    C. II, IV, V
    D. III, IV, V

13. Which one of the following occurred under the Soviet New Economic Policy?

    A. Soviet collectivization of farms made great strides.
    B. Middlemen were removed from private trading.
    C. The big individualist farmers (Kulaks) became less important.
    D. Peasant proprietors engaged in capitalistic agriculture.

14. Which one of the following occurred during the Eisenhower Administration?

    A. Nikita Khrushchev became the dictator of the Soviet Union.
    B. Congress passed the McCarran Immigration and Nationality Act.
    C. The Castro Regime was declared incompatible with the principles of the Organization of American States.
    D. The 22nd Amendment was ratified by the required 36 states.

15. Prior to the nuclear test ban treaty of 1963, the LAST written agreement signed by the Union of Soviet Socialist Republics and the United States was the

    A. United Nations Charter
    B. Peace Treaty with Japan
    C. Peace Treaty with Austria
    D. Potsdam Agreement

16. Which one of the following is TRUE of the Hungarian Uprising of 1956?
    It

    A. proved that the Uniting for Peace Resolution had made the General Assembly more effective
    B. provided a rare instance of United States and Russian cooperation in the United Nations
    C. demonstrated Soviet willingness to permit a Titoist-type of regime in Hungary
    D. showed that a disagreement between the United States and the former Union of Soviet Socialist Republics could paralyze action in the General Assembly

17. *Red Sunday* is a term referring to the slaughter of

    A. Girondists in the French Revolution
    B. peasants in Russia's Revolution of 1905
    C. Huguenots in the French religions war
    D. Nazis in the first *beer-hall putsch*

18. Nicolai Lenin's New Economic Policy provided for the

    A. relinquishment of state ownership of basic industries
    B. suppression of big individual farmers or kulaks
    C. substitution of a *planned economy* for the remnants of free enterprise
    D. restoration of private enterprise for profit

19. Between the end of World War II and 1965, the United States and the Soviet Union agreed upon all of the following EXCEPT the

    A. conclusion of an Austrian peace treaty
    B. formation of a treaty on Antarctica
    C. condemnation of the Anglo-Grench-Israeli attack on Egypt in 1956
    D. assessment on United Nations members to support United Nations Congo military operations

20. In which one of the following pairs is there NO causal relationship between the two items?

    A. War of the Austrian Succession - Decembrist Revolt
    B. The Crimean War - Reforms of Alexander II
    C. The Russo-Japanese War - Revolution of 1905
    D. World War I - Revolution of 1917

21. One reason for the improvement of Russian-British relations after 1892 was that

    A. the Triple Alliance brought a period of peace in Europe
    B. Russia supported Great Britain in the Egyptian crisis of 1882
    C. Great Britain supported Russia at the Congress of Berlin in 1878
    D. Russia settled her differences with England over Afghanistan and Persia

22. Which one of the following constituted a violation by the Soviet Union of agreements made at the Yalta Conference?

    A. Acquiring the Kurile Islands from Japan
    B. Entering the war against Japan
    C. Preventing free democratic elections in Eastern Europe
    D. Occupying the eastern zone of Germany

23. In which one of the following treaties did Russia NOT participate?

    A. Re-insurance Treaty of 1887
    B. Dual Alliance of 1894
    C. Entente Cordiale of 1904
    D. Triple Entente of 1907

24. Which one of the following historical items is NOT matched correctly with the country with which it is MOST closely associated?

    A. Third Force - France
    B. Fabianism - England
    C. Splendid Isolation - Russia
    D. Young Plan - Germany

25. Which one of the following suffered the GREATEST territorial loss in Europe after World War I?

    A. Austria-Hungary   B. Germany
    C. Russia   D. Turkey

KEY (CORRECT ANSWERS)

1.	D	11.	B
2.	B	12.	B
3.	B	13.	D
4.	A	14.	A
5.	C	15.	C
6.	D	16.	D
7.	B	17.	B
8.	C	18.	D
9.	C	19.	D
10.	A	20.	A

21. D
22. C
23. C
24. C
25. C

TEST 5

DIRECTIONS: Each question or incomplete statement is followed by several suggested answers or completions. Select the one that BEST answers the question or completes the statement. *PRINT THE LETTER OF THE CORRECT ANSWER IN THE SPACE AT THE RIGHT.*

1. Which is the CORRECT chronological order of the following events?
    I. Communist coup in Czechoslovakia
    II. Communist victory on China mainland
    III. Communists gain control of Poland
    IV. Russia blockades West Berlin
   The CORRECT answer is:

   A. III, I, IV, II
   B. III, I, II, IV
   C. III, II, I, IV
   D. None of the above

   1.____

2. In June 1950, the Security Council of the United Nations was able to act quickly to brand North Korea the aggressor because the

   A. General Assembly happened to be in session
   B. Soviet Union was boycotting its meetings
   C. veto does not apply in the case of armed conflict
   D. President of the United States had already ordered American armed forces to support South Korea

   2.____

3. Which one of the following pairs is NOT in a cause-and-effect relationship?

   A. The Napoleonic Wars - Decembrist Revolt
   B. The Crimean War - Reforms of Alexander II
   C. The Russo-Japanese War - Revolution of 1905
   D. World War I - Revolution of 1917

   3.____

4. In which one of the following ways did the Bolsheviks secure power in Russia? By

   A. overthrowing the Czar
   B. being voted into office by the all-powerful Soviets
   C. staging a coup d'état against the Provisional government
   D. making a united front with the Mensheviks in the Constituent Assembly

   4.____

5. Which one of the following was one of the provisions of the Yalta Agreement of 1945?

   A. It restored to the Union of Soviet Socialist Republics the imperialist rights the Czar had lost in the Far East.
   B. In recognition of the Soviet losses in the war, the Soviet Union was granted the option of joining the fight against Japan.
   C. It gave the Russians eight votes in the United Nations General Assembly to counterbalance the votes of the British Commonwealth.
   D. It provided for the recognition of the Soviet-controlled Polish government by Franklin D. Roosevelt and Winston Churchill.

   5.____

6. In which one of the following are the events arranged in CORRECT chronological order?
   I. Russo-Japanese War
   II. Sino-Japanese War
   III. Japan's annexation of Formosa
   IV. Russia's getting concession in Liaotung Peninsula

   The CORRECT answer is:

   A. II, I, IV, III
   B. III, IV, I, II
   C. II, III, IV, I
   D. IV, II, I, III

7. Which one of the following economic concepts was developed by Karl Marx?

   A. Conspicuous consumption
   B. Cooperatives
   C. Industrial democracy
   D. Surplus value

8. The government which was the FIRST to gain power with the fall of the Tsar of Russia was the

   A. Constituent Assembly dominated by the Social Revolutionaries and Mensheviks
   B. government established by Lenin
   C. government under Kerensky's leadership
   D. provisional government under Lvov

9. Of the following, the statement which BEST illustrates a basic principle held by Karl Marx is that

   A. the needs of citizens can best be satisfied within the family unit
   B. government is essential to guarantee the rights of the individual
   C. class differences lead to social conflict
   D. people should be rewarded primarily according to their contributions and achievements

10. From 1949 to the development of Nixon's policy of détente, the leaders of mainland China have viewed United States policy as one of encirclement and a threat to the existence of the People's Republic. This view was a result of

    A. United States support of the Nationalists on Taiwan, involvement in the wars in Korea and Vietnam, and the presence of military bases in Japan and the Philippines
    B. United States policies such as the Marshall Plan and NATO which were designed to reconstruct and rebuild Western Europe as a bulwark against Russian expansion
    C. the failure of the United States and its allies to prevent the Russians from enforcing the Brezhnev Doctrine in Czechoslovakia
    D. the United States policy of exporting nuclear technology for economic purposes only and its refusal to accept unilateral nuclear disarmament

11. The term that BEST characterizes the foreign policy of the United States since World War II is

    A. appeasement
    B. isolationism
    C. containment
    D. non-intervention

12. Stalin's 1939 non-aggression treaty with Hitler was intended to provide   12._____

    A. Stalin with time to consolidate his power in Russia and avoid an invasion against his unprepared nation
    B. Russia with much needed technical and capital equipment to assure success of the Five Year Plan for industrialization
    C. the world with another respite from the prospect of World War II
    D. Russia greater leverage in its negotiations with Britain and France for a collective security pact

13. The Russian Constitution of 1906   13._____

    A. set up an elected parliament called the Duma
    B. established Alexander Kerensky as premier
    C. granted all citizens equality before the law
    D. provided for emancipation of the serfs

14. In the Russo-Chinese Pact of 1945, the Soviet government agreed to   14._____

    A. give military supplies and moral support to the Nationalist government
    B. recognize Chinese rule over Outer Mongolia
    C. support the Chinese Communists in their fight to gain control of China
    D. give China complete control of the Chinese Eastern Railway

15. Which of the following statements is TRUE concerning Russia's foreign relations?   15._____

    A. After the American Revolution, Russia was the first power to recognize the United States as a sovereign power.
    B. Russia refused to cooperate with the Quintuple Alliance in suppressing the liberal uprisings in Latin America.
    C. During our Civil War, Russia sent her fleets to the harbors of New York and San Francisco.
    D. Russia agreed to submit the Bering Sea controversy to arbitration.
    E. Russia forced Japan to restore Shantung to China after the Sino-Japanese War.

16. All of the following are true of present-day life in Russia EXCEPT   16._____

    A. allowing prices to rise to market level
    B. an increase in literacy
    C. a ban on the services of the Eastern Orthodox Church
    D. the encouragement of private enterprise
    E. the right to own personal property

17. The U.S.S.R. had attempted to secure control of or gain rights in all of the following ports   17._____
    EXCEPT

    A. Petsamo   B. Dairen   C. Bergen
    D. Vladivostok   E. Port Arthur

18. Which of the following statements were TRUE concerning communism in Russia before the breakup of the Soviet Union?
    I. Less than 10% of the Russians were members of the Communist party.
    II. Russians may own their homes and personal belongings.
    III. The Constitution (1936) guaranteed freedom of speech, press, assembly, and conscience.
    IV. Differential wages were paid.
    V. Most peasants were members of cooperative groups.

    The CORRECT answer is:

    A. I, II, IV, V
    B. I, III, IV, V
    C. I, V
    D. II, IV
    E. All of the above

19. Which of the following events occurred LAST?

    A. Stalin succeeded Lenin as titular head of the Communist party in the U.S.S.R.
    B. Churchill succeeded Chamberlain as Prime Minister of Great Britain.
    C. Mussolini assumed power as dictator of Italy.
    D. Franklin D. Roosevelt was elected President of the United States for the first time.
    E. Chiang Kai-shek assumed leadership of the Nationalist movement in China.

20. During World War II, the straits at the entrance to the Black Sea were controlled by

    A. Bulgaria
    B. Germany
    C. Great Britain
    D. Russia
    E. Turkey

21. Pravda was the name of a Russian

    A. censor
    B. editorial writer
    C. newspaper
    D. radio network
    E. war reporter

22. All of the following statements express policies of the United States government during the Cold War EXCEPT:

    A. Our policy with regard to Europe was not to interfere with her internal concerns but to consider each European government de facto as the legitimate government and to cultivate friendly relations with it
    B. Even though Soviet leaders professed to believe that the conflict between capitalism and communism was irreconcilable and must eventually be resolved by the triumph of the latter, was our hope that a fair and equitable settlement would be reached when they realize that we were too strong to be beaten and too determined to be frightened
    C. If we find it impossible to enlist Soviet cooperation in the solution of world problems, we should be prepared to join with the British and other Western countries in an attempt to build up a world of our own
    D. The role of this country should consist of friendly aid in the drafting of a European economic program to get Europe on its feet and to provide financial support for such a program so far as it may be practical for us to do so
    E. The United States seeks no territorial expansion or selfish advantage and has no plans for aggression against any other state, large or small, but is committed to the mutual security of non-Communist nations in Europe

23. One of the MOST widely publicized policies of the State Department, the policy of *containment,* was attributed to George F. Kennan.
Of the following, the MOST correct statement of this policy is that

    A. the encroachments of the Russians can be halted by helping nations to develop their economies and thus raise their standards of living
    B. the Russians should be confronted with unalterable counterforce at each point where they show signs of encroaching upon the interests of a peaceful and stable world
    C. containment is not possible unless the Russians are made to understand that further encroachments will result in an American attack on Russia itself
    D. the United States should ally itself with any country, no matter what its government is, provided that it is willing to join in preventing Russia from expanding
    E. imperialist Russia can be contained by providing the free world with the means of defense

23.____

24. In 1948, the neo-Lamarckian views of a previously obscure Russian scientist, Lysenko, were officially adopted by the U.S.S.R.
According to scientists outside the *Iron Curtain* countries, the position taken by Lysenko was NOT correct because it assumes that

    A. acquired characteristics, those induced by environment and habit, are inherited in kind
    B. a series of determiners for a developmental system is acquired after birth
    C. evolution is ultimately inexplicable because it is a matter of cellular consciousness
    D. individual adaptation to environment occurs during the prenatal period
    E. the type of individual which develops depends upon the interplay of inherited determiners, activities of the organism, and the environment during development

24.____

25. There is here a stark reality upon which our foreign policies must be based. With any foreseeable land forces from non-Communist nations, even including the United States, a land offensive against the Communist world could bring no military victory, no political conclusion ...our foreign policies must be based on the defense of the Western Hemisphere.
This statement represented MOST NEARLY the viewpoint of

    A. Charles Bohlen   B. Dean Acheson
    C. Dwight D. Eisenhower   D. Herbert Hoover
    E. Thomas E. Dewey

25.____

KEY (CORRECT ANSWERS)

1. A
2. B
3. A
4. C
5. A

6. C
7. D
8. D
9. C
10. A

11. C
12. A
13. A
14. C
15. C

16. C
17. C
18. E
19. B
20. E

21. C
22. A
23. B
24. A
25. D